A BIBLIOGRAPHY OF THE SANSKRIT DRAMA

A BIBLIOGRAPHY OF THE SANSKRIT DRAMA

WITH AN INTRODUCTORY SKETCH OF THE DRAMATIC LITERATURE OF INDIA

MONTGOMERY SCHUYLER

GYAN

Published by

Gyan Publishing House
5, Ansari Road
Daryaganj, New Delhi-110002
Phone: 011-47034999, 9811692060
E-mail: books@gyanbooks.com

Distribution Network
gyanbooks.com
India, USA, Canada, UK, Australia, France

ISBN : 9788121231497 (PB)
First Published, 1906

2nd Impression 2020

Printed at: Gyan Press, Delhi.

A Bibliography of the Sanskrit Drama
Author: Montgomery Schuyler

A BIBLIOGRAPHY

OF THE

SANSKRIT DRAMA

WITH AN

INTRODUCTORY SKETCH OF

THE DRAMATIC LITERATURE OF INDIA

BY

MONTGOMERY SCHUYLER, Jr., A.M.

SECRETARY OF LEGATION AND CONSUL-GENERAL OF THE UNITED STATES TO SIAM
SOMETIME FELLOW IN INDO-IRANIAN LANGUAGES
IN COLUMBIA UNIVERSITY

New York
THE COLUMBIA UNIVERSITY PRESS
THE MACMILLAN COMPANY, Agents
66 FIFTH AVENUE
1906

TO

PROFESSOR A. V. WILLIAMS JACKSON

MY FRIEND AND TEACHER

To make future editions of the bibliography more nearly complete and accurate, all persons observing errors or omissions are requested to communicate them to the editor of this series, A. V. Williams Jackson, Columbia University, New York, who will gratefully acknowledge all such assistance.

PREFACE

It has long been desirable that students of Sanskrit literature should have as complete a catalogue as possible of all Hindu authors and their writings, in order that they might be able to tell at a glance how many manuscripts of each work are known, how many editions and translations have been made, and what has been written concerning them. It is the purpose of the present volume to fill this need for the Sanskrit drama. The material here presented has been collected for several years, but unforeseen circumstances have delayed the publication long beyond the time originally proposed, although some portions of the work have already appeared in print.[1]

In a book of this character it is practically impossible to secure absolute completeness, and this is especially true of lists of manuscripts, since new catalogues of collections both in India and in Europe are constantly being published.[2] Many titles of earlier editions and of the older ancillary literature, moreover, were accessible to me only in catalogues of various descriptions, frequently compiled with scant regard to bibliographical accuracy and by no means complete. The conditions under which I labored precluded the possibility of access to all the actual manuscripts and editions, and I was therefore obliged to cite a large number of entries at second or even at third hand. Absolute fidelity to the original titles has consequently been denied me, and — a far more serious matter — it has only too often proved impossible for me to secure the pagination and other details of very practical import for Sanskritists. Even when the volumes were at hand, however, I did

[1] In JAOS. 22 (1901), pp. 237–248; 23 (1902), pp. 93–103; 25 (1904), pp. 189–196; Verhandlungen des 13. internationalen Orientalisten-Kongresses (1902), Leiden, 1904, pp. 33–37.

[2] In fact, Hz. 3 and IO. 7 were received while the volume was passing through the press, and the references to these were added in the proofs by Mr. Haas.

not think it necessary to reproduce all the padding with which native scholars adorn their title-pages, so that a long entry has frequently been abridged in the following pages to the simple phrase 'edited with notes by . . .'

The arrangement of names and titles follows the order of the English alphabet, and no separate positions have been assigned to the vowels and consonants distinguished by diacritical marks. **Heavy-faced type** is used for the names of playwrights, ordinary Roman type for the names of plays. Plays are inserted under the author's name, when it is known, and cross-references are given under the titles of his various works. Anonymous plays are listed under the names by which they are known. Some titles, although identical with those of works by known authors, have had to be recorded in like manner as anonymous, merely because the necessary data for a determination of their authorship were not available. For the same reason no exact statement as to the number of extant dramas can be made at the present time.

Such honorific designations as 'Śrī,' 'Kavi,' 'Bhaṭṭa,' 'Paṇḍita,' and 'Rāja' have usually been omitted, unless they form a part of the name as commonly known or are necessary to avoid confusion with some other playwright of the same appellative. Editions and translations are arranged as far as possible in chronological order, critical works are classified alphabetically by authors. Volumes containing both text and translation are listed under text editions, and critical essays and notes are not separately recorded under critical works when included in editions of the text or in translations. Criticism relating entirely to a single author or play is catalogued under that author or play, but general books and papers are separately listed before the main body of the bibliography. A reference such as 'Amṛtodaya, A 1. p. 29' indicates that Aufrecht in his Catalogus Catalogorum has listed on that page one manuscript of a play called Amṛtodaya. When more than one manuscript is referred to, the number is given. In the case of commentaries the number of manuscripts is also stated. Thus 'Com. 5, by Jagaddhara 2' indicates that there are five manuscripts of unspecified or anonymous commentaries and two manuscripts of a commentary by Jagaddhara. In this way each entry shows the number of extant manuscripts of the work and of the various commentaries on it, if such exist. Some entries from Part 7 of the India Office Catalogue, however, duplicate those already given by Aufrecht from the Catalogue of the Mackenzie Collection; these were added because the early catalogue of Wilson gives no adequate description of the manuscripts, and because it seemed desirable to include all material not given by Aufrecht. The same is true of the Catalogue of Two Collections in the India Office Library, by Tawney and Thomas, which includes manuscripts recorded by Aufrecht from an old list by Sir William Jones. An introductory sketch of the Sanskrit drama has been incorporated in the volume, in order that students may have a convenient epitome of the whole subject readily accessible to them.

For the manuscripts listed in this bibliography I have relied in the main on the marvelously accurate and learned Catalogus Catalogorum of Aufrecht, although I have supplemented it by such catalogues as have appeared subsequently. For many titles of editions of plays and records of literature on the drama of India I am indebted to the bibliographies of Gildemeister and Zenker and to the Catalogue of Sanskrit books in the British Museum, although my richest source has naturally been the Orientalische Bibliographie. Antiquarian catalogues, especially those of Harrassowitz (Leipzig) and Luzac (London), have also been consulted with advantage.

My thanks are due to the librarians of the Royal Libraries of Copenhagen and Stockholm for information in regard to certain publications, while through the kindness of Professor Serge Oldenburg of St. Petersburg I had access to the large collections of the Russian Academy of Sciences and the Oriental Seminar of the University of St. Petersburg, and certain queries were answered for me by Professor Carl Cappeller of Jena. My friend and former fellow-student, Dr. Louis H. Gray, placed his library at my disposal and gave me several additions and suggestions, while both he and Mrs. Gray most generously aided in the correction of the proofs. The main part of this toilsome revision, however, which my absence from America compelled me to forego, has been most kindly undertaken for me by Mr. George C. O. Haas, Fellow in Indo-Iranian in Columbia University, who has also added the new material from Hultzsch's Reports and the India Office Catalogue, and made many corrections and improvements. To my friend and teacher, Professor A. V. Williams Jackson, who, from the inception of the book to its completion, has grudged neither time nor pains to aid me, my deepest gratitude is due for his inspiration and assistance.

MONTGOMERY SCHUYLER, JR.

UNITED STATES LEGATION,
BANGKOK, SIAM,
November 1, 1905.

CONTENTS

INTRODUCTORY SKETCH OF THE SANSKRIT DRAMA

It is now more than a hundred years since Sir William Jones gave the Western world its first knowledge of the dramatic literature of the Hindus by the publication, in 1789, of a translation of the *Śakuntalā* of Kālidāsa. From that time on, the labors of Sanskritists have gradually made accessible most of the chief works of the Sanskrit drama, and a large number of editions, translations, and commentaries are now available for the general student of literature.

Origin.

The earliest manifestations of a dramatic idea in India are to be found in the hymns of the Rig Veda. Certain of these hymns are in the form of dialogues between various personages of the Vedic pantheon, such as Yama and Yamī, Saramā and the Paṇis, while the myth of King Purūravas and the nymph Urvaśī is the foundation for one of the plays of India's greatest dramatist. The lack of accurate data precludes our knowing much about the origin of the drama in India, but it is probable that it had its beginning in a combination of these hymns in dramatic form and in the religious dances, in which certain pantomimic features came to be conventionalized and stereotyped in later times until we get the classical Sanskrit drama. This theory is borne out by the fact that in Sanskrit the words for play (*nāṭaka*) and actor (*naṭa*) are from the root *naṭ* which is the Prākrit form of the Sanskrit *nṛt* 'to dance.' The native Hindu account of the origin of the drama was that it came down from heaven as a fully developed art invented by the divine sage Bharata. This theory, however satisfying to the Hindu mind, cannot be accepted by modern scholarship, and we are forced to presuppose a development from the religious to the dramatic, as outlined above, which is not essentially different from that found in Greece. The earlier stages, which were connected with religious festivals, and especially with the worship of Kṛṣṇa-Viṣṇu, were not unlike the early primitive Christian mystery-plays of the Middle Ages in Europe.

Whatever may have been its beginnings, it is certain that the drama flourished in India, and had a high development. The earlier plays as we know them had considerable freedom of choice of subject and treatment and they can be described, for the most part, as melodramas or tragicomedies. Primarily their elements are mixed: gravity and gaiety, despair and joy, terror and love—all are combined in the same play. Tragedy, in our sense of the term, there is none, for every drama must have a happy ending. As, according to the rules, death cannot be represented on the stage, it follows that one great source of inspiration for European tragedy is entirely eliminated. The usual subject for dramatic treatment is love, and according to the rank or social position of the hero and heroine the play is placed in one or another of the ten chief (*rūpaka*) or eighteen minor (*uparūpaka*) divisions of the drama recognized by the Hindu text-books.[1] The trials and tribulations of the lovers, relieved by the rather clumsy attempts at wit of the *vidūṣaka*, or court jester, the plotting of the *viṭa*, or parasite, and the efforts of the rival wives to establish themselves in the favor of their lords and masters, with the incidents of every day life in the harem and court, constitute the plot of the play. The laments of the hero to his confidant, the jester, serve to introduce lyrical stanzas descriptive of the beauties of nature, the wiles and graces of woman, and the tender passion which fills the hero's heart for some fair maiden or celestial nymph. According to the Sanskrit treatises on dramatic art the subject of a *nāṭaka* is to be taken from some famous legend, and its hero must be high-minded and

Character.

[1] Although the drama is so carefully subdivided by the rhetorical text-books, not all of these divisions are represented in the extant literature (see Appendix II). The precise character of many of the plays here recorded, however, could not be determined, as most manuscript cataloguers fail to distinguish the various varieties and use the word 'nāṭaka' in the general sense of 'drama.' It is to be hoped that future cataloguers will examine the plays with more care and so record them that we may get a better idea of the comparative popularity of the different forms of drama.

of noble birth, sprung from a race of gods or kings.[1] The expression of all feelings is allowed, but preponderance is to be given to love and heroism. There must be not less than five, nor more than ten, acts of mingled prose and verse. The Sanskrit tongue itself, as the learned or court language, is spoken by gods, Brahmans, heroes, kings, and men of good birth and position in general. Women and the lower classes of men speak various dialects of the Prākrit language, the old vernacular tongue of India. Among the Prākrits the most important is the Śaurasenī, the form usually found in the dramas, the Mahārāṣṭrī being confined to the poetical stanzas.[2] The rules for distinguishing the various individual kinds of characters are all carefully classified and divided; so far does this subdividing go that no less than three hundred and eighty-four types of heroine are given. In practice, of course, this is never carried out, but it must be acknowledged that the great defect of the Sanskrit drama is that in general it is too conventional, with the result that originality and life are sacrificed for a hackneyed arrangement and a stereotyped manipulation of threadbare sentiments and action.

Plots and Dramatis Personae.

In the invention of plots the dramatists show little fertility of imagination; on the other hand cleverness is certainly clearly shown in the way in which the details of the plot are worked out and the development of the intrigue is presented. In the majority of cases the plot is somewhat as follows: the hero, who is usually a king or a prince and already has one or more wives, at the opening of the play suddenly becomes enamored of the charms of some girl or nymph. Although she is equally in love with him she is too bashful and modest to let her passion be observed. Hope and fear alternately cheer and dismay both hero and heroine. She confides in some girl friend, he in the jester, who is always a brahman, but a person of slow intelligence whose uncouth attempts at wit seem often lacking in every element of humor. The jester,

[1] NŚ. 19.117; SD. 277; DR. 3.1, 34.

[2] See Pischel, Grammatik der Prakrit-Sprachen, § 30; NŚ. 17.31-44; SD. 432; DR. 2.59, 60.

moreover, is a glutton, greedy for money, and, as is to be expected, an inveterate gossip, always on the watch for some fresh bit of news. One of the most curious features of the Sanskrit drama, fostered as it was by the court society of India, which was almost always under the control of brahman priests, is that this figure of a degraded and besotted brahman should be allowed to appear as a typical stage-figure. In an article written some years ago[1] I advanced the theory that such a seeming inconsistency might be due to the fact that the drama had its origin in the religious dances and ceremonies of the common people, who were of course largely non-brahmanic, and was therefore an outgrowth of the many popular religions of India rather than a development of pure brahmanism. In this way the conventional figures, having become in the course of time crystallized into permanent types, were retained when the folk-drama became popular at court, and thus even brahman authors did not hesitate to perpetuate the type, though really derogatory to their class. Other stock characters in the plays are the parasite (*viṭa*), ministers, Buddhist monks and nuns, servants of the harem, dwarfs, mutes, and the female attendants of the king.

Technical Divisions and Arrangement of a Play.

For the technical divisions of a drama and the development of the plot there are carefully elaborated rules, but of the actual scenic arrangement of a play, the manner of producing it, and the assignment of the roles we know comparatively little. Plays seem to have been usually presented at the spring festival. A drama always opens with a *nāndī*, or benediction, usually addressed to Śiva, for the prosperity of the audience, by the *sūtradhāra*, or director. This director must have been very accomplished and versatile, for the rules say that among other things he must know music, technical treatises, dialects, the art of managing, works on poetry, rhetoric, acting, industrial arts, metre, astronomy, geography, history, and the genealogies of royal families. He was to have a good memory, and to be honest, intelligent, dignified, and

[1] The origin of the Vidūṣaka and the employment of this character in the plays of Harṣadeva, in JAOS. 20 (1899), pp. 338–340.

noble. According to the text-books he had two associates: the *sthāpaka* and the *pāripārśvika*.[1] It is probable that in the actual practice of the theatre the duties assigned by the treatises to the *sthāpaka* were all performed by the *sūtradhāra*.[2] At the end of the *nāndī* there is a dialogue between the manager and some actor complimenting the audience on their critical ability and ending by introducing one of the characters of the play, after which the action goes on with regular divisions into acts and scenes. Scenes are marked by the exit of one person and the entrance of another, as on the Classical and the French stage, and the stage is never left empty until the end of the act. Between the acts a connecting scene called *viṣkambhaka* is often introduced, in which occurrences that have taken place since the preceding act are explained. The theory of the unity of time, place, and action, which played so important a part in the Greek drama, appears in rather a modified form in India. The time of the action is supposed to be the same as that occupied in the performance, or else to fall within twenty-four hours. But this rule is not always observed, and we find in the *Uttararāmacarita* of Bhavabhūti a lapse of twelve years between the first and second acts. Unity of place is not strictly observed, and journeys are often made, sometimes even through the air in celestial cars.

Theatre and Scenery.

As to the stage-setting and decoration very little is yet known. Special buildings for the presentation of plays are described in the *Nātyaśāstra*,[3] but it is probable that dramas were usually given in a hall (*saṃgīta-śālā* 'concert-room') of the palace. Behind the stage, which occupied a quarter of the whole hall,[4] was a curtain divided in the middle, and behind that again was the greenroom (*nepathya*) whence the actors came on the stage. The greenroom had an entrance from the outside 'separate from the entrance for the audience.'[5] Scenery and

[1] DR. 3. 3; SD. 283.

[2] But Lanman believes with Konow that the *Karpūramañjarī* of Rājaśekhara shows the *sthāpaka* in action. See the edition and translation of the play by Konow and Lanman, pp. 196, 223, note 8.

[3] NŚ. 2. 1 seq. See also Bloch, ZDMG. 58 (1904), pp. 455–457.

[4] NŚ. 2. 37.

[5] NŚ. 2. 85.

decoration were apparently very simple and much was left to the imagination. Elaborate directions for gestures, pantomime, and clothing are given. Thrones, seats, chariots, weapons, and armor were employed, and some sort of mechanical contrivances were perhaps not unknown. We must infer, however, from the frequent use of the word *nāṭayitvā*, 'having gesticulated,' *nāṭayati*, 'mimics, acts as if doing,' as a stage direction, that pantomime and gesticulation were largely resorted to for filling out the deficiencies of the staging.

Age of the Drama of India.

The age of the Sanskrit drama may roughly be given as extending from 400 to 1100 A.D. This period does not, of course, include the earliest efforts at dramatic composition, nor take in a large number of late and inferior plays. Very little is known of the earliest dramatists before Kālidāsa, and none of their compositions excepting scattered verses are extant. For example, the poets Bhāsa, Rāmila, Somila (or Saumillaka), and the Kaviputras were well known and popular playwrights among the Hindus of Kālidāsa's time, but our knowledge of them is practically confined to their names.[1]

Śūdraka's Mṛcchakaṭikā.

Most students of the Sanskrit drama are of the opinion that the *Mṛcchakaṭikā*, or 'Clay Cart,' of Śūdraka is the oldest extant Sanskrit play. The arguments in favor of this view are based upon the state of civilization shown in the play, the general style of the drama and the richness and diversity of the Prākrit dialects employed in its composition. Some scholars, however, whose researches in the Hindu drama entitle them to speak with great authority upon this subject, believe that the play is not earlier than the sixth century of our era, or approximately of the same period as Kālidāsa's dramas. I must confess, nevertheless, that I find myself among the number of those that are inclined to consider it of much earlier date. The question of the authorship of the *Mṛcchakaṭikā* is also still under discussion. In the prologue the play is stated

[1] See the prologue to Kālidāsa's *Mālavikāgnimitra*, and F. Hall in JASBe. 28 (1859), p. 28 seq., and in the introduction to his *Vāsavadattā*, pp. 14–15.

to be the production of King Śūdraka, but not all kings are authors, and it is thought that in this case, as probably in others, the real author, like a wise courtier, may have attributed his work to his royal master in order to gain favor. Many of the rulers of ancient India delighted in playing the part of patrons of art and literature; Śūdraka may well have been one of these. Professor Pischel, after a careful study of the material, thinks that the real author was a poet named Daṇḍin. However that may be, there is no question that the *Mṛcchakaṭikā* is in many respects the most human of all the Sanskrit plays. There is something strikingly Shaksperian in the skilful drawing of the characters, the energy and life of the large number of personages in the play, and in the directness and clearness of the plot itself. It is a ten-act *prakaraṇa*, or comedy of middle-class life, and the scene is laid in the city of Ujjain. The subject of the plot is the love and marriage of Carudatta, a brahman merchant reduced to poverty by his generosity, and Vasantasenā, a rich courtesan. In the third act there is a long and humorous account of a burglary in which stealing is treated as an art or science provided with rules and conventional procedure. The chief value of the *Mṛcchakaṭikā*, aside from its interest as a drama, lies in the graphic picture it presents of a very interesting phase of everyday life in ancient India. The elaborate description of the heroine's palace in the fourth act gives us a glimpse of what was considered luxury in those days. The name 'Clay Cart' is taken from an episode in the sixth act, which leads to the finding of the heroine's jewels in the terra cotta cart of the hero's little son and to their use as circumstantial evidence in a trial. This complicates the plot until all is resolved in the *dénouement*.

Kālidāsa.

The greatest name in Sanskrit literature is that of Kālidāsa who lived at the court of Ujjain, probably about the first half of the sixth century of our era, although his date is not settled and the question is still a mooted one. He is the author of three plays, *Śakuntalā*, *Vikramorvaśī*, and *Mālavikāgnimitra*. The first two of these compositions reach the highest level attained by the Hindu dramatists and win for their author a place among the greater poets of the world. Their richness of fancy and appreciation of nature, added to the beauty of poetic technique and choice of language, have never been equaled in India, and bear favorable comparison with the dramas of any nation.

The play of *Śakuntalā* has been known in Europe since its translation by Sir William Jones in 1789, by which work that great Orientalist really introduced Sanskrit poetry to the West and started the study of Hindu literature. The play is a *nāṭaka*, or heroic comedy, of seven acts, and its plot is drawn from the first book of the *Mahābhārata*. The subject of the drama is the love of King Duṣyanta for Śakuntalā, their separation by accident, and their ultimate reunion in the presence of their son after the lapse of some years. The importance of this play lies not only in the fact that it is the most perfect Sanskrit drama extant, but also in the fact that its great literary merit, as was evident from Sir William's translation, aroused a widespread interest in the literature of India throughout Europe. It was enthusiastically received by the followers of the Romantic School and exercised a genuine influence upon them. Jones's English version was soon rendered into other languages, and independent translations from the original Sanskrit have since been made into almost all the tongues of Europe, so that I am able to record versions and adaptations of the play in English, German, French, Italian, Spanish, Dutch, Danish, Swedish, Icelandic, Russian, Polish, Hungarian, and Bohemian.

Kālidāsa's other important play is the *Vikramorvaśī*. It was first translated into English into 1827 by Horace Hayman Wilson, a scholar who devoted a great part of his life to the study of the Sanskrit drama, and whose 'Select Specimens of the Theatre of the Hindus' is a standard work even to-day. Later investigations have rendered some of his views antiquated, but his book remained for years the only work upon the Sanskrit drama as a whole, until the appearance, in 1890, of Sylvain Lévi's admirable and scholarly treatise, *Le Théâtre indien*, a work indispensable to students. The plot of the *Vikramorvaśī* is briefly as follows: King Purūravas rescues the nymph Urvaśī, who has been carried away by the demons, and his heroism wins her love. The lovers become separated by accident, but after various vicissitudes are reunited in the presence of their son when the latter is about twelve years old.

The third play of Kālidāsa, entitled *Mālavikāgnimitra*, or 'King Agnimitra's Love for Mālavikā,' is a conventional drama of harem intrigue at the court, and is decidedly inferior to the author's other two plays. So marked is this inferiority that some scholars have even gone so far as to question its right to bear Kālidāsa's name.

Harṣadeva.

We now come to an interesting group of three plays ascribed to Harṣadeva, king of northern India, which have been the object of much discussion. As in the case of the *Mṛcchakaṭikā*, it is probable that they were the work of some poet who, to curry favor, ascribed their authorship to that famous patron of art and literature, Harṣadeva. These three plays are *Ratnāvalī*, *Priyadarśikā*, and *Nāgānanda*. The first two are dramas of harem intrigue and court life, composed, it is true, upon conventional lines, but showing some ingenuity in the manipulation of plot and the invention of incident. In the *Ratnāvalī*, or 'Jewel Necklace,' the subject is the story of the loves of Vatsa, or Udayana, king of Kauśāmbī, and Sāgarikā, an attendant of his wife, queen Vāsavadattā, who ultimately is discovered, by a necklace she wears, to be Ratnāvalī, princess of Ceylon, who had been shipwrecked and had found her way to Vatsa's court. The characters are clearly defined and not mere puppets, as in the case of some dramas. The poetical part is rather conventional, but there are several pretty lines descriptive of natural scenery, moonrise, and the like. The drama *Priyadarśikā*, named after its heroine, is much the same sort of play, but not so good. The lack of a good critical edition and English translation of this play has made it difficult for students, but this lack is soon to be overcome, and a translation by G. K. S. Nariman, with an introductory memoir from the pen of Professor Jackson, will soon be ready. The third play, *Nāgānanda*, 'Joy of the Serpents,' is in some respects quite unique. It is a highly-colored melodrama with a pronounced Buddhistic tendency, as Buddha is invoked in the *nāndī*, and the hero himself is a Buddhist. In this respect the *Nāgānanda* stands alone among the extant Sanskrit plays, although we know that there were other Buddhist dramas which have not been preserved. Such was the *Lokānanda* of Candragomin, of which there is a Tibetan translation. The *Nāgarāja* and *Śānticarita* are, perhaps, imitations of the *Nāgānanda* or even identical with it. In the *Avadānaśataka* (75) there is a record of the representation of a Buddhist drama, according to Oldenburg.[1] Several Jain plays are also known.[2]

Bhavabhūti.

The dramatist Bhavabhūti, who lived during the first half of the eighth century, was a native of Vidarbha, the Province of Berar, in south-central India, and he wrote under the protection of king Yaśovarman of Kanauj. He is the author of three plays, the *Mālatīmādhava*, *Mahāvīracarita*, and *Uttararāmacarita*, which are distinguished by great poetic beauty and feeling, exquisite verse, polished style, but little humor or wit (the jester being absent from all), and only moderate dramatic power. They are, perhaps, dramatic poems rather than dramas. Bhavabhūti's home in the mountain regions of south-central India doubtless gave him a love of the grand and titanic aspects of nature instead of the mild and gentle phases described by the other Hindu authors. His characters have much grace and tenderness and also possess energy and life. His most popular play is the ten act *prakaraṇa*, or melodrama, *Mālatī-mādhava*, the scene of which is laid in Ujjain. It is the story of the love of Mālatī, daughter of a cabinet minister, and Mādhava, a young student. This charming play is often called the *Romeo and Juliet* of India, but it has a happy ending, as all Sanskrit plays must have. The whole drama is a succession of contrasted situations, first of love and then of the weird incantations of the terrible priestess of Durgā, scenes which are used to heighten the dramatic effect as well as to contribute to

[1] In Zapiski Vostočnago Otdĕleniya Imp. Russkago Arkheologičeskago Obščestva, 4 (1890), pp. 393-394.

[2] See Lévi p. 324.

the plot. In the fifth act the scene is laid in the field where the bodies of the dead are burned. The two other plays of Bhavabhūti form a history of the deeds of the hero Rama, and are based on the epic poem *Rāmāyaṇa*. I shall omit a detailed description of these.

The next dramatist, Rājaśekhara, who lived about the year 900 A. D., is the author of four plays which have come down to us. Two of them are much like the comedies of Harṣadeva in construction and subject. These two are the *Viddhaśālabhañjikā*, or 'The Lady of the Statue' and the *Karpūramañjarī*, or 'Camphor Cluster.' They are both dramas of harem and court life. The chief interest of the *Karpūramañjarī*, which has been admirably edited in the Harvard Oriental Series by Dr. Sten Konow with a translation by Professor Lanman, consists in the fact that it renders accessible the only extant example of the kind of drama called *saṭṭaka*. The *saṭṭaka* is nearly the same as the *nāṭikā*, or minor heroic comedy, except that it is composed entirely in Prākrit. Of the *Viddhaśālabhañjikā* I had hoped to publish a translation, upon which I was engaged, but the pressure of other duties has prevented me, and the work has now been done by my friend and fellow-student, Dr. Louis H. Gray.

Rājaśekhara.

One of the few historic plays of India is the *Mudrārākṣasa* by Viśākhadatta. The scene of this elaborate drama is laid in the city of Pāṭaliputra during the reign of Candragupta, or shortly after the invasion of India by Alexander. The time of composition of the play, however, is probably to be placed about the year 1000 A. D. The plot deals with the story of the founding of a new dynasty by Candragupta who had deposed the former ruler. The latter's minister Rākṣasa refuses to recognize the new monarch. Candragupta's minister tries to win Rākṣasa over to his own political plans, which are well conceived, and he at last succeeds. The drama gives us a remarkable picture of the political conditions of the time in which the author has placed its action, centuries before his own.

Viśākhadatta.

Nārāyaṇa Bhaṭṭa. The *Veṇīsaṃhāra*, or 'Binding of the Braid,' by the playwright Nārāyaṇa Bhaṭṭa, is a six-act drama based on the incident of the *Mahābhārata* in which the Pāṇḍu wife Draupadī is dragged by the hair into the assembly and outrageously exposed before the Kurus. The play is written in exact accordance with the rules of text-books and largely for that reason it has always been a favorite in India.

Kṣemīśvara. An admirable but less known drama is the *Caṇḍakauśika* by Kṣemīśvara, whose date is uncertain. This play presents a vivid picture of the workings of a curse uttered by the angry priest Kauśika against an upright king who had innocently offended him. The king forfeits his realm and loses his wife and child, the latter by death and his consort by her being sold into slavery. Though tried to the utmost, the Job-like patience of the righteous monarch never fails, and in the end he has his wife, his son, and his kingdom restored to him by divine intervention, so that all ends in happiness.

The Mahānāṭaka. In the eleventh century was composed a dramatic monstrosity, the huge *Mahānāṭaka*, ascribed to Hanuman, the monkey-king. It has fourteen acts in one recension and ten in the other, and thus violates the rule which requires that no drama shall exceed ten acts in length. It is quite without interest to students of literature except as a curiosity.

Kṛṣṇamiśra. The tenth and eleventh centuries in India witnessed a renewed interest in the dramatic art, and to that time belong many other plays which must be omitted here on account of lack of space. One, however, which must be mentioned is the *Prabodhacandrodaya*, or 'Rise of the Moon of Intellect,' an allegorical drama by the poet Kṛṣṇamiśra. The characters in this play, as in the old English Moralities, are symbolical figures and personified abstract ideas, and it is indeed remarkable that with such subject matter the author should have succeeded in producing a drama of so much real merit. The plot is as follows: The wicked King Error is the ruler of the city of Benares. He is surrounded by his followers, the Follies and Vices, while the good King Reason and his followers, Religion and the Virtues, have been sent into exile. In accordance with a prophecy, Reason will at some time marry Revelation, and the fruit of that union will be True Knowledge, who will overthrow the power of King Error. The plot recounts the vicissitudes of the struggle and the final triumph of good.

The *Saṃkalpasūryodaya* of Veṅkaṭanātha and the *Caitanya-candrodaya* of Kavikarṇapūra who wrote about the middle of the sixteenth century are obvious imitations of the *Prabodhacandrodaya* and have as dramatis personae almost the same characters.

Of the later history of the Sanskrit drama it is not necessary to write at length. It has had a continuous existence from the period of the greatest works down to the present time.[1] The later plays, although written in exact accordance with the rules of Hindu dramaturgy, are for the most part lacking in interest and action.

Later Plays.

[1] Wilson in 1827 gave the names of 60 Sanskrit plays, Lévi in 1890 was able to increase the number of titles known to 372, and the present bibliography lists over 500 separate productions.

ABBREVIATIONS

A1, A2, A3.	= Aufrecht, T., Catalogus Catalogorum. Pts. 1, 2, 3. Leipzig, 1896–1903.
Cat. Mack. Coll.	= The Mackenzie Collection. A descriptive catalogue of the Oriental Manuscripts, by H. H. Wilson, 2° ed., Madras, 1882.
CBMMS.	= Catalogue of the Sanskrit Manuscripts in the British Museum, Cecil Bendall. London, 1902.
CS.	= Sanskrit Manuscripts in the Calcutta Sanskrit College, by Śāstrī and Gui, no. 18, Calcutta, 1903.
DR.	= Daśarūpa, edited by F. Hall, Calcutta, 1865.
Ep. Ind.	= Epigraphia Indica.
Garbe	= Verzeichniss der indischen Handschriften der kōniglichen Universität zu Tübingen, von Richard Garbe, Tübingen, 1899.
Hz. 3.	= Reports on Sanskrit Manuscripts in Southern India, by E. Hultzsch, no. 3, Madras, 1905.
IA.	= Indian Antiquary.
JA.	= Journal Asiatique.
JAOS.	= Journal of the American Oriental Society.
JASBe.	= Journal of the Asiatic Society of Bengal.
JRAS.	= Journal of the Royal Asiatic Society.
JRASBo.	= Journal of the Royal Asiatic Society, Bombay Branch.
L.	= Lévi, Sylvain, Le Théâtre indien, Paris, 1890.
NŚ.	= Nāṭyaśāstra, edited by Śivadatta and Parab, Bombay, 1894. Cf. also the edition of Grosset, Paris, 1898.
RS.	= Rasārṇavasudhākara by Śiṅgabhūpāla. [A list of works mentioned in this is given in SRep. p. 10]

SCBen. = Sanskrit, Jain, and Hindi Manuscripts in the Sanskrit College, Benares. Allahabad, 1902.

SD. = Sāhityadarpaṇa, edited and translated by Ballantyne and Mitra. Calcutta, 1875, 2 vols. [The references are to sections.]

SRep. = Report on a Search for Sanskrit and Tamil Manuscripts for 1896–7, by M. S. Sastri. Madras, 1898.

TT. = Catalogue of two collections of Sanskrit Manuscripts preserved in the India Office Library. Compiled by C. H. Tawney and F. W. Thomas. London, 1903.

Weber = Handschriften-Verzeichnisse der königlichen Bibliothek, Bd. 1. Verzeichniss der Sanskrit-Handschriften, von A. Weber. Berlin, 1853.

Wilson = Select Specimens of the Theatre of the Hindus. London, 1871, 2 vols.

WZKM. = Wiener Zeitschrift für die Kunde des Morgenlandes.

ZDMG. = Zeitschrift der Deutschen Morgenländischen Gesellschaft.

GENERAL WORKS ON THE SANSKRIT DRAMA

1. Hindu Works on Dramatics.

Abhinayadarpaṇa A 1. p. 24 = 4 Mss.

Bharata.

Nāṭyaśāstra. *Manuscripts.* A 1. p. 284 = 3 Mss.; A 2. p. 61 = 1 Ms. and 1 Com.; A 3. p. 61.

Text Editions. Nāṭyaśāstra. Edited by Śivadatta and Parab. Bombay, 1894, pp. 3 + 447. Kāvyamālā, no. 42.

Nāṭyaśāstra. Traité de Bharata sur le théâtre. Texte Sanskrit. Édition critique. Avec une introduction, les variantes tirées de quatre manuscripts, une table analytique et des notes par Joanny Grosset. Précédée d'une préface de Paul Regnaud. Tome I. Première partie = Annales de l'Université de Lyon. fasc. 40, Paris, 1898, pp. 12 + 27 + 296.

Nāṭyaśāstra, adhyāyas 18, 19, 20, 34. Published by F. Hall in his edition of the Daśarūpa, Calcutta, 1865, pp. 199–241.

Contribution à l'étude de la musique hindoue par J. Grosset. Paris, 1888, pp. 91. In Bibliothèque de la Faculté des Lettres de Lyon, vol. 6. [Text of bk. 28 of the Nāṭyaśāstra with translation and notes.]

Le 17me chapitre du Bhāratīya Nāṭyaśāstra intitulé Vāg-Abhinaya, publié pour la première fois par P. Regnaud. In Annales du Musée Guimet, 1 (1880), pp. 85–99.

La Métrique de Bharata. Text Sanscrit de deux chapitres du Nāṭya-śāstra, publié pour la première fois et suivi d'une interprétation française par Paul Regnaud. In Annales du Musée Guimet, 2 (1881), pp. 63–130. [End of chapter 15 and chapter 16.]

Nāṭyaśāstra. Sixth and seventh chapters, edited with notes and variants by Paul Regnaud, in his Rhétorique Sanskrite, Paris, 1884, part 2, pp. 1–42.

Criticism. Nāṭyaśāstra. Traité sur le théâtre publié par J.

Grosset. Préface (par P. Regnaud) et introduction. Lyon, 1897, pp. 40.

Dhruva, H. H., Nāṭyaśāstra, or the Indian dramatics. In As. Quart. Rev. 2 (1896), pp. 349–359.

Dhanaṃjaya.

Daśarūpa. *Manuscripts.* A 1. pp. 247–248 = 16 Mss. and 1 Com.; by Dhanika 9, by Nṛsiṃha Bhaṭṭa 1, by Pāṇi 1; A 2. p. 53 = 7 Mss. and Com. by Kuravirāma 1, by Dhanika 7, by Devapāṇi 1.

Text Editions. Daśarūpa or Hindu canons of dramaturgy, with the exposition of Dhanika, the Avaloka. Edited by F. Hall. Calcutta, 1865, pp. 39 + 241. In Bibl. Indica.

Daśarūpa with the commentary of Dhanika. Edited by J. Vidyāsāgara. Calcutta, 1878, pp. 230.

Daśarūpa. With the commentary of Dhanika. Edited by K. P. Parab. Bombay, 1897, pp. 153.

Hastamuktāvalī A 1. p. 764.

Nandin Abhinayadarpaṇa A 1. p. 24 = 7 Mss.; A 3. p. 6 = 3 Mss.

Idem Abhinayadarpaṇa. Poona, 1874.

Nāṭakacandrikā A 2. p. 61.

Nāṭakalakṣaṇa A 2. p. 61.

Nāṭakaratnakośa cf. A 1. p. 284.

Nāṭakāvatāra cf. A 1. p. 284.

Nāṭasūtra (?) cf. A 1. p. 284.

Nāṭyadarpaṇa cf. A 1. p. 284.

Nāṭyalakṣaṇa A 1. p. 284.

Nāṭyalōcana A 3. p. 61.

Nāṭyaśāstra A 1. p. 284.

Puṇḍarīka Nāṭakalakṣaṇa A 1. p. 284.

Rūpa Gosvāmin Nāṭakacandrikā alaṃkāra A 1. p. 284 = 2 Mss.; A 2. p. 207.

Rāmacandra Nāṭyadarpaṇa A 3. p. 61.

Śiṅgadharaṇīśa Nāṭakaparibhāṣā A 1. p. 284; A 2. p. 61.

Śrīkaṇṭhaka Rasakaumudī Nāṭyaśāstre A 1. p. 494.

Sundaramiśra (1613) Nāṭyapradīpa mentioned in DR. intr. p. 1.
Trilocanāditya Nāṭyalocana A 1. p. 284 = 2 Mss. and 1 Com.
Tryambaka Nāṭakadīpa A 1. p. 284 = 1 Ms. and 3 Com.; by Rāmakṛṣṇa 1.
Vasantarāja Nāṭyaśāstra mentioned by Mallinātha on Śiśupālavadha 2. 8; cf. A 1. pp. 284, 556.

Viśvanātha Kavirāja.

Sāhityadarpaṇa. *Manuscripts.* A 1. p. 715 = 21 Mss. and 4 Com.; by Mathurānātha Śukla 1, by Rāmacaraṇa 7; A 2. pp. 171, 233 = 3 Mss. and Com. by Anantadāsa 1, by Rāmacaraṇa 2; A 3. p. 148 = 5 Mss. and Com. by Rāmacaraṇa 2; Hz. 3. 1750.
Text Editions. Sāhityadarpaṇa. Edited by Nātha Rāma. Calcutta, 1828.
Sāhityadarpaṇa. The text revised by E. Roer, Calcutta, 1851.
Sāhityadarpaṇa. The Mirror of Composition. Edited and translated by Ballantyne and Mitra. Calcutta, 1875, 2 vols.
Sāhityadarpaṇa. Edited by J. Vidyāsāgara. 1° ed., Calcutta, 1874; 3° ed., 1890, pp. 702; 5° ed., 1900, pp. 630.
Sāhityadarpaṇa. With a commentary. Annotated and edited by D. Dviveda and K. P. Parab. Bombay, 1902, pp. 644.
Criticism. Alaṃkāravādārtha, a discussion on the Sāhityadarpaṇa. A3. p. 7.

2. WORKS OF GENERAL CRITICISM.

Analyse d'un monologue dramatique indien. Paris, 1850.
Das indische Theater. In Globus, 49 (1886), pp. 380–381.
Baumgartner, Alexander. Geschichte der Weltliteratur, vol. 2., 3° ed., Freiburg im Breisgau, 1902, pp. 134–203.
Bloch, Th. Ein griechisches Theater in Indien. In ZDMG. 58 (1904), pp. 455–457.
Böhme, R. Indische Dramatik. In Vossische Zeitung, 1903, Sonntagsbeilage, no. 37.

Cappeller, Carl. Zwei Prahasanas. In Gurupūjākaumudī, Festgabe für Weber, Leipzig, 1896, pp. 59–63.

Cimmino, Francesco. Il tipo comico del "vidūshaka" nell' antico dramma indiano. In Atti della Reale Accademia di Archeologia, Lettere e Belle Arti (di Napoli), 15 (1893), pp. 97–142.

Cimmino, Francesco. Il teatro indiano in Europa. Communicazione letta al Congresso di Parigi nel 1897. Naples, 1897.

Cimmino, Francesco. Studii sul teatro indiano. 1. Sul dramma Karpūramañjarī. 2. Sul dramma Caṇḍakauśika. In Rendiconto della Reale Accademia di Archeologia, Lettere e Belle Arti (di Napoli), 19 (1905), pp. 1–76.

Colizza, Giovanni. Del riconoscimento nel dramma indiano e nel dramma greco. Rome, 1897, pp. 105. [Treats only Śakuntalā and Oedipus Rex.]

Druskowitz, A. Shakespeare's Vorläufer in Indien und andere indische Dramatiker. In Dramaturgische Blätter und Bühnenrundschau, 17 (1888), pp. 638–639.

Gubernatis, Angelo de. Storia universale della letteratura, vol. 1, pp. 19–110; vol. 2, pp. 11–108. Milan, 1882–1883.

Gray, Louis H. Literary Studies on the Sanskrit Novel, 2. The Sanskrit Novel and the Sanskrit Drama. In WZKM. 18 (1904), pp. 48–58.

Hall, F. Fragments of three early Hindu dramatists, Bhāsa, Rāmila, and Somila. In JASBe. 28 (1859), pp. 28–30.

Herder, J. G. von. Über das Morgenländische Drama. In Werke zur Schönen Literatur und Kunst, Stuttgart, 1828.

Hertel, Johannes. Der Ursprung des indischen Dramas und Epos. In WZKM. 18 (1904), pp. 59–83, 139–168.

Hillebrandt, Alfred. Zur Charakteristik des indischen Drama's (1888). In his Alt-Indien, Breslau, 1899, pp. 147–167.

Huizinga, J. De Vidūṣaka in het indisch Tooneel. Groningen, 1897, pp. 155.

Jackson, A. V. Williams. Children on the Stage in the Sanskrit Drama. In Proc. Am. Philol. Assoc., 27 (1896), pp. v, vi. [Abstract of the following article.]

Jackson, A. V. Williams. Children on the Stage in the Ancient Hindu Drama. In the Looker-On, New York, June 1897, vol. 5, no. 6, pp. 509–516.

Jackson, A. V. Williams. Certain Dramatic Elements in Sanskrit Plays with Parallels in the English Drama. First series. In Am. Journ. Philol., 19 (1898), pp. 241–254.

Jackson, A. V. Williams. Disguising on the stage as a dramatic device in Sanskrit plays. In Proc. Am. Philol. Assoc., 29 (1898), pp. 18–19.

Jackson, A. V. Williams. Time Analysis of Sanskrit Plays. 1. The Dramas of Kālidāsa; 2. The Dramas of Harsha. In JAOS. 20 (1899), pp. 341–359, and 21 (1900), pp. 88–108.

Κεφαλλῆνος, Μ. Αἱ ἑλληνίδες ἑταῖραι ἐν τῷ ἰνδικῷ δράματι. Athens, 1886. [Considers only the Mṛcchakaṭikā.]

Kern, H. Een blik op het indisch Tooneel. In De Gids, 1898, pp. 466–496.

Kielhorn, F. Sanskrit plays preserved as inscriptions. In Academy, 1891, p. 67; JRAS. 1891, pp. 165–166. See also app. to Ep. Ind. 5 (1899), p. 20.

Kielhorn, F. Sanskrit plays partly preserved as inscriptions at Ajmere. In IA. 20 (1891), pp. 201–212.

Kielhorn, F. Bruchstücke indischer Schauspiele in Inschriften zu Ajmere. In Festschrift z. Feier d. 150jähr. Bestehens d. Kgl. Gesellschaft d. Wiss. zu Göttingen, Berlin, 1901, pp. 30.

Klein, J. L. Das indische Drama, in his Geschichte des Dramas, vol. 3, Leipzig, 1866, pp. 1–373.

Lévi, Sylvain. Le Théâtre indien. Paris, 1890, pp. 15 + 432 + 125. [The standard work on the Sanskrit drama.]

Lévi, Sylvain. Sur quelques termes employés dans les inscriptions des Kṣatrapas. In JA. 9° series, 19 (1902), pp. 95–125.

Leumann, Ernst. Eine Bitte an die künftigen Herausgeber von Dramen und nichtvedischen Prosa-Texten der indischen Literatur. In ZDMG. 42 (1888), pp. 161–198.

Oldenburg, S. F. Ukazaniye na predstavleniye buddiskoi dramy. In Zapiski Vostočnago Otdĕleniya Imp. Russkago Arkheologičeskago Obščestva, 4 (1890), pp. 393–394. [Mention of a representation of a Buddhist Drama. Text from the Avadānaśataka (75).]

Ongaro, Prof. Dall'. Studii critici sul teatro indiano. In Rivista Europea, Florence, Jan. 1873.

Hariścandra. Nāṭaka: on drama in Sanskrit and Hindi with sketch of European drama. Benares, 1883, pp. 54. [In Hindi.]

Nève, F. Les drames héroiques et mythologiques de l'Inde. In Muséon, 1 (1882), pp. 523–540.

Nevill, Hugh. The Rāmāyaṇa as a Play. In Taprobanian, 2 (1887), pp. 150–160, 170–172.

P[avolini], P. E. Sul personaggio del Vidūṣaka. In Studi italiani di filologia indo-iranica, edited by Pulle, 2 (1899), pp. 86–87. [A review of Huizinga's work, De Vidūṣaka in het indisch Tooneel.]

Pischel, Richard. Die Heimat des Puppenspiels. Hallesche Rektorreden, 2, Halle, 1900, pp. 28.

[Pischel, Richard.] The Home of the Puppet Play. Translated by Mildred C. Tawney. London, 1902, pp. 32.

Sāradānanda (Swami). Poetry and Drama of Ancient Times. In Brahmavadin, 3 (1897), pp. 346–355.

Schuyler, Montgomery, Jr. The Origin of the Vidūṣaka, and the employment of this character in the plays of Harṣadeva. In JAOS. 20 (1899), pp. 338–340.

Sladomel, Ig. Dramatické umění indu. In Vlast, 13 (1897), pp. 835–845.

Smith, Vincent A. The Reign of Harsha from 606 to 648 A. D. In his Early History of India, Oxford, 1904, pp. 282–302.

Tagore, S. M. Bhāratīya Nāṭya Rahasya, or a Treatise on Hindu Drama. Calcutta, 1878, pp. 268. [In Bengali.]

Tagore, S. M. The Hindu Drama, 1. Calcutta, 1888, pp. 56.

Windisch, E. Der griechische Einfluss im indischen Drama. In Verh. d. 5. intern. Orientalisten-Kongresses (1881), sect. 2, Berlin, 1882, pp. 3–106.

Winternitz, Moritz. The Mahābhārata and the drama. In JRAS. 1903, pp. 571–572.

Zubaty, Josef. On the development of the Indian drama and its relation to the Greek drama [in Bohemian]. In Listy filologike of Prague, 14 (1887), pp. 1–7; 98–108; 193–205. [Chiefly on the hetairai of the Hindu and the Greek drama.]

3. Chapters in Histories of Sanskrit Literature.

Frazer, R. W. A Literary History of India. London and New York, 1898, pp. 263–299.

Henry, Victor. Les Littératures de l'Inde. Paris, 1904, pp. 274–320.

Macdonell, Arthur A. A History of Sanskrit Literature. London and New York, 1900, pp. 346–367.

Lassen, Christian. Indische Alterthumskunde, vol. 2, 2° ed. Leipzig, 1874, pp. 506–514, 1170–1174; vol. 4, 1861, pp. 817–821.

Manning, Mrs. C. S. Ancient and Mediaeval India, vol. 2, London, 1869, pp. 141–288.

Oldenberg, H. Die Literatur des alten Indien. Stuttgart and Berlin, 1903, pp. 236–281.

Schroeder, Leopold von. Indiens Literatur und Cultur. Leipzig, 1887, pp. 591–666.

Weber, Albrecht. Vorlesungen über indische Literaturgeschichte. 2° ed., Berlin, 1876–78, pp. 213–225.

Weber, Albrecht. History of Indian Literature. Translated from the Second German edition by J. Mann and Th. Zachariae. 2° ed., London, 1882, pp. 196–208.

Williams, Monier. Indian Wisdom. 3° ed., London, 1876, pp. 462–489.

4. Collected Translations of Sanskrit Dramas.

Fritze, Ludwig. Indisches Theater, Sammlung indischer Dramen in metrischer Übersetzung. Schloss-Chemnitz, 1877–79, 3 vols.

Marazzi, Antonio. Teatro scelto indiano, tradotto dal sanscrito. Milan, 1871–74, 2 vols. (vol. 1, Teatro di Calidasa; vol. 2, Mudrārāxasa e Dhūrtasamāgama).

Wilson, Horace Hayman. Select Specimens of the Theatre of the Hindus, translated from the original Sanskrit. Appendix containing short accounts of different dramas. 1° ed., Calcutta, 1826–27, 3 vols.; 2° ed., London, 1835, 2 vols.; 3° ed., London, 1871, 2 vols. (in Works of H. H. Wilson, vols. 11, 12); reprinted, Calcutta, 1902, 2 vols.

Langlois, A. Chefs-d'oeuvres du théâtre indien, traduits de l'original sanscrit en anglais, par H. H. Wilson, et de l'anglais en français; accompagnés de notes et d'éclaircissemens, et suivi d'une table alphabétique des noms propres. Paris, 1828, 2 vols.

[Wolff, O. L. B.] Theater der Hindus. Aus der Englischen Übersetzung des Sanskrit-Originals metrisch übersetzt. Weimar, 1828–31, 2 vols.

NAMES OF AUTHORS AND TITLES OF THEIR WORKS.

A

Abhijñānaśakuntalā *see* **Kālidāsa.**

Abhinavagupta, a dramatic critic, mentioned in SD. 506.

Abhinavarāghavānanda *see* **Maṇika.**

Abhirāmamaṇi *see* **Sundara Miśra.**

Adbhutadarpaṇa *see* **Mahādeva.**

Adbhutarāghava *see* **Vanamāli.**

Adbhutaraṅga prahasana A 1. p. 8.

Adbhutārṇava *see* **Kavibhūṣaṇa.**

Aditikuṇḍalāharaṇa *see* **Kādamba.**

Ahalyāsaṃkrandana A 1. p. 37.

Aindavānanda *see* **Rāmacandra Kavi.**

Ambāla *see* **Varadācārya.**

Ambikādatta Vyāsa Sāmavata, an original drama in six acts on the Pauranik legend of Sāmavān. Preceded by an essay on the dramatic art and accompanied by short notes by Babunandana and followed by a Prākrit-Sanskrit glossary. Bankipur, 1888, pp. 19 + 139 + 14.

Ammāl Vedāntavilāsa A 1. p. 29.

Amogharāghava mentioned in RS.

Amṛtacandra Sūri Samayasāra L. app. p. 81.

Amṛtodaya A 1. p. 29.

Amṛtodaya *see* **Gokulanātha.**

Ānandadhara Mādhavānala A 1. p. 450 = 2 Mss.; A3. p. 97

Ānandakośa prahasana mentioned in RS.

Ānandalatikā *see* **Kṛṣṇanātha.**

Ānandarāghava *see* **Cūḍāmaṇi.**

Ānandarāya *see* **Vedakavisvāmin.**

Ānandarāya Makhin, son of Nārāyaṇa or Nṛsiṃharāya (A 2 p. 9), wrote about 1780, Jīvānandana A 2. p. 201.

Idem Jīvānandana. Edited by Durgāprasāda and Parab Bombay, 1891, pp. 3 + 108. Kāvyamālā, no. 27.

Idem Vidyāpariṇaya A 1. p. 574; A 2. p. 225; A 3. p. 121.
Idem Vidyāpariṇayana. Edited by Śivadatta and Parab. Bombay, 1893, pp. 3 + 88. Kāvyamālā, no. 39.
Ānandasundarī saṭṭaka A 1. p. 49.
Ānandasundarī *see* **Ghanaśyāma.**
Ānandatilaka bhāṇa A 1. p. 46.
Anaṅgabrahmavidyāvilasa *see* **Varadācārya.**
Anaṅgajīvana *see* **Varada.**
Anaṅgalatikā L. app. p. 73.
Anaṅgalekhā mentioned in Alaṃkāravimarśinī.
Anaṅgamaṅgala *see* **Sundara Kavi.**
Anaṅgasaṃjīvana *see* **Varada.**
Anaṅgasarvasva *see* **Lakṣmīnṛsiṃha.**
Anaṅgavijaya *see* **Jagannātha Paṇḍita.**
Anantadeva, son of Āpadeva, Kṛṣṇabhakticandrikā A 1. p. 121 = 9 Mss.; A 2. p. 28 = 3 Mss.; A 3. p. 27 = 4 Mss.
Idem Kṛṣṇabhakticandrikā, a short drama in 177 verses with prose interspersed. Poona, 1878–88. In Kāvyetihāsasaṃgraha, 4, nos. 10–12.
Anantarāma Svānubhūtyabhidha A 1. p. 752.
Anargharāghava *see* **Murāri.**
Aṅgada *see* **Bhūbhaṭṭa.**
Añjanāpavanaṃjaya *see* **Hastimalla.**
Antaravyākaraṇa *see* **Kṛṣṇānanda.**
Anutāpāṅka quoted in SD. 481.
Appāśāstrin Lavalīpariṇaya A 1. p. 543.
Idem Sārasvatādarśa A 1. p. 714.
Appayya Dīkṣita Vasumatīcitrasenāvilāsa A 1. p. 557.
Arjunarāja *see* **Hastimallasena.**
Aruṇagirinātha Yogānanda prahasana A 1. p. 481; A 2. p. 177 = 2 Mss.; A 3. p. 151. This play is called in A 2. Somavallīyogānanda.
Aśvamedha *see* **Sumatijitāmitramalladeva.**
Atandracandrika *see* **Jagannātha** *and* **Vidyānidhi.**
Atirātrayājin (16th century) Kuśakumudvatīya A 1. p. 113.

B

Badhyaśilā *see* Vadhyaśilā.

Bālabhārata *see* **Rājaśekhara.**

Bālacarita quoted in SD. 346.

Bāla Kavi Gairvanivijaya. The triumph of Sanskrit. A short allegorical play, referring to the foundation of Sanskrit schools in Travancore. Palghat, 1890, pp. 12.

Bālakṛṣṇa Muditarāghava A 2. p. 106.

Bālarāmāyaṇa *see* **Rājaśekhara.**

Bālivadha preṅkhaṇa mentioned in SD. 547.

Bāṇa Bhaṭṭa (7th century), son of Citrabhānu.

Mukuṭatāḍitaka mentioned by Caṇḍapāla on Damayantīkāvya (p. 227). Cf. L. app. p. 78.

Pārvatīpariṇaya. *Manuscripts.* A 1. p. 336 = 13 Mss.; A 3. p. 72; Hz. 3. 1849.

Text Editions. Pārvatīpariṇaya. Herausgegeben von Prof. K. Glaser. In Sitzungsb. der kais. Akad. der Wiss. (zu Wien), 104 (1883), pp. 578–612.

Pārvatīpariṇaya. Edited by M. R. Telang. Bombay, 1892, pp. 48.

Pārvatīpariṇaya. Edited with commentary, notes, and translation by T. R. Ratnam Aiyar. Kumbhakonam, 1898, pp. 214.

Translations. Parvati's Hochzeit. Ein indisches Schauspiel übersetzt von Dr. K. Glaser. (Separatabdruck aus dem Jahresbericht des K. K. Staats-Gymnasiums in Trieste, 1886, pp. 9 + 38.)

Pārvatī Pariṇaya, translated from Sanskrit into Marathi by P. B. Godbole. Poona, 1869; new ed., revised by V. P. Shāstrī, Bombay, 1872, pp. 160.

Criticism. Glaser, K. Über Bāṇa's Pārvatīpariṇaya. In Sitzungsb. der kais. Akad. der Wiss. (zu Wien), 104 (1883), pp. 575–664. [Cf. also the review by Fritze, in Literatur-Blatt für Orientalische Philologie, 1 (1884), pp. 184–185.]

Telang, K. T. The Pārvatīpariṇaya of Bāṇa. In IA. 3 (1874), pp. 219–221.

Bāṇa Bhaṭṭa Sarvacarita A 1. p. 701.
Bhagavadabjaka quoted in Rucipati's commentary on the Anargharāghava of Murāri (ed. of Durgāprasāda and Parab, p. 7).
Bhagavadajjukā prahasana mentioned in RS.
Bhagavantarāya Rāghavābhyudaya A 2. p. 117.
Bhāgavata Kṛṣṇakavi Śarmiṣṭhāyayāti A 1. p. 638.
Bhaimīpariṇaya A 1. p. 416 = 9 Mss. and 1 Com.
Bhaimīpariṇaya *see* **Ratnakheṭa, Śaṭhakopācārya,** *and* **Veṅkaṭācārya.**
Bhairavaprādurbhāva L. app. p. 78.
Bhānumātīpariṇaya (?) L. app. p. 78 (but cf. A 1. p. 405).
Bhānuprabandha *see* **Veṅkaṭeśa.**
Bharadvāja Kāleyakutūhala prahasana A 1. p. 396.
Idem Kāleyakutūhala. Poona, 1882, pp. 32. In Kāvyetihāsasaṃgraha, 5, nos. 2–5.
Bharatarāja *see* **Hastimallasena.**
Bhartṛharinirveda *see* **Harihara.**
Bhartṛmeṇṭha, a Kashmirian playwright of the sixth century (cf. A 1. p. 397).
Bhāsa Svapnavāsavadattā, mentioned in prologue to Mālavikāgnimitra of Kālidāsa. Cf. F. Hall, Fragments of three early Hindu dramatists, in JASBe. 28 (1859), pp. 28–30.
Bhāskara Unmattarāghava A 1. p. 66.
Idem Unmattarāghava. A drama in prose and verse in one act, on the story of Rāma. Bombay, 1889, pp. 3 + 16. Kāvyamālā, no. 17. [Reprinted from an edition published in Palamanair by S. S. Śāstri.]
Bhaṭṭa Nārāyaṇa *see* **Nārāyaṇa.**

Bhavabhūti (end of seventh century).

Mahāvīracarita. *Manuscripts.* A 1. p. 443 = 29 Mss. and 3

Com. ; by Ātmārāma 1, by Vīrarāghava 1 ; A 2. pp. 102, 217 = 7 Mss. and Com. by Vīrarāghava 2 ; CS. 242 ; Hz. 3. 1575; IO. 7. 4135, 4136. Analyzed by Wilson, 2, pp. 323–334.

Text Editions. Mahāvīracarita, or the history of Rama, edited by F. H. Trithen. London, 1848, pp. 4 + 147.

Mahāvīracarita. Edited by T. Tarkavācaspati with occasional glosses. Calcutta, 1857, pp. 2 + 120.

Mahāvīracarita. Edited with notes by J. Vidyāsāgara. Calcutta, 1873, pp. 142.

Mahāvīracarita. Edited by Anundoram Borooah, with a Sanskrit commentary and a Sanskrit-English glossary. Calcutta and London, 1877, pp. 13 + 310.

Mahāvīracarita, edited with various readings and notes in Sanskrit by S. G. Jyotishi. Poona, 1887, pp. 135 + 29.

Mahāvīracarita, with the commentary of Vīrarāghava, edited by T. R. Ratnam Aiyar, S. Rangachariar, and K. P. Parab. 1° ed., Bombay, 1892, pp. 260; 2° ed., 1901, pp. 260.

Mahāvīracarita, a Sanskrit drama, with the commentaries of Lakṣmaṇa Sūri. New ed., Madras, 1904, pp. 270.

Translations. Mahāvīracarita. The Adventures of the Great Hero Rāma. An Indian Drama in seven acts. Translated into English prose from the Sanskrit by John Pickford. London, 1871, pp. 16 + 172. Reprinted 1892, pp. 20 + 172.

Mālatīmādhava prakaraṇa. *Manuscripts.* A 1. p. 453 = 62 Mss. and Com. by Jagaddhara 11, by Tripurāri Sūri 10, by Mānāṅka 3, by Rāghava Bhaṭṭa 1, a condensed version by Maithila Śarman 1 ; A 2. p. 104 = 7 Mss. and Com. by Jagaddhara 1, by Tripurāri 1, by Nārāyaṇa 1, Prākṛtachāyā 1 ; CS. 243, 244; IO. 7. 4125, 4126, 4127, 4128, 4129, 4130; TT. 61 ; Com. by Jagaddhara, SCBen. 430, IO. 7. 4130, 4131, 4132 ; Com. by Mānāṅka, IO. 7. 4130, 4133 ; condensed version by Maithila Śarman, IO. 7. 4134.

Text Editions. Mālatīmādhava, with a commentary of the. Prākrit passages. Calcutta, 1830, pp. 175.

Malatimadhavae fabulae actus primus cum variis lectionibus edidit C. Lassen. Bonn, 1832, pp. 48.

·Mālatīmādhava, with a translation of the Prākrit passages, edited by K. C. Dutt. Calcutta, 1866, pp. 148.

Mālatīmādhava, with the commentary of Jagaddhara, edited with notes, critical and explanatory, by R. G. Bhandarkar. Bombay, 1876, pp. 399 + 76. Bombay Sanskrit Series, no. 15.

Mālatīmādhava, edited with a commentary by J. Vidyāsāgara. Calcutta, 1876, pp. 185.

Mālatīmādhava, with the commentary of Tripurārisūri called Bhāvapradīpika, in Telugu. Madras, 1883, pp. 176 + 128.

Mālatīmādhava. Saṭīka. Part 1. Calcutta, 1886, pp. 60.

Mālatīmādhava, with the commentary of Jagaddhara, edited with an interpretation of the Prākrit passages by Bhuvanacandra Vasāka. Calcutta, 1886, pp. 317.

Mālatīmādhava, with the commentaries of Tripurāri and Jagaddhara, edited by M. R. Telang. 1° ed., Bombay, 1892, pp. 402; 2° ed., 1900, pp. 402.

Translations. A. English. Malati and Madhava, or the Stolen Marriage, translated by Wilson, 2, pp. 1–123.

B. French. Madhava et Malati. Drame traduit du sanscrit et du pracrit par G. Strehly, précédé d'une préface par A. Bergaigne. Paris, 1885, pp. 12 + 274. Bibl. Orient. Elzévir., no. 42.

C. German. Malatimadhava, ein indisches drama von Bhavabhuti. Zum ersten Male aus dem Original ins Deutsche übersetzt von Ludwig Fritze. Leipzig, 1883, pp. 125.

D. Dutch. Malati en Madhava. Een indisch drama vertaald en verkort door P. A. S. van Limburg Brouwer. In Tijdspiegel, 1871, i, 418.

E. Bengali. Malatee Mudhaba, a comedy of Bhubabhootee. Translated into Bengalee from the original Sanskrit, by K. P. Sing. Calcutta, 1859.

F. Marathi. Mālatīmādhava. Translated into Marathi by K. S. Rajvade and revised by Chiplonkar. Bombay, 1861, pp. 152.

Uttararāmacarita. *Manuscripts.* A 1. p. 63 = 67 Mss. and 3 Com.; Bhāvārthadīpika 1, by Nārāyaṇa 7, by Rāghavācārya 3, by Vīrarāghava 1; A 2. p. 190 = 2 Mss. and Com. by Nārāyaṇa 1; A 3. p. 14 = 5 Mss. and Com. by Abhirāma 1; CS. 219; Hz. 3. 1607; Com. by Ghanaśyāma, Hz. 3. 1600; Com. by Nārāyaṇa, CS. 220, SCBen. 81, IO. 7. 4137.

Text Editions. Uttararāmacarita, with a commentary explanatory of the Prākrit passages. Calcutta, 1831, pp. 132.

Uttararāmacarita. Edited, at the request of [and with a preface by] E. B. Cowell, by Premacandra Tarkabagisa. With a short commentary. Calcutta, 1862, pp. 181.

Uttararāmacarita, edited with commentary by Tarakumara Cakravarti. With a preface by B. P. Majumdar. Calcutta, 1870, pp. 208.

Uttararāmacarita. Edited with Sanskrit notes by Iśvaracandra Vidyāsāgara. 3° ed. (?), Calcutta, 1876, pp. 15 + 246.

Uttararāmacarita, with a commentary called Bhāvabodhi by Ramacandra Budhendra. Madras, 1881. [In Grantha characters.]

Uttararāmacarita, with extracts from two Sanskrit commentaries and notes in English by K. B. Mande. Poona, 1881, pp. 75 + 17.

Uttararāmacarita. Edited by J. Vidyāsāgara. 1° ed., Calcutta, 1881; 2° ed., 1889, pp. 268.

Uttararāmacarita, edited with copious Sanskrit and English notes by S. G. Bhanap. 1° ed., Bombay, 1888, pp. 212; 2° ed., 1893, pp. 218.

Uttararāmacarita, with Sanskrit commentary by Pandit B. S. Ghate, together with a close English translation and notes by V. S. Patvardhan. Nagpur, 1895, 12 + 192 + 47.

Uttararāmacarita. With the commentary of Vīrarāghava. Edited by T. R. Ratnam Aiyar and K. P. Parab. 1° ed., Bombay, 1899, pp. 174; 2° ed., 1903, pp. 174.

Uttararāmacarita. Sanskrit text with a commentary by Lakṣmaṇa Sūri. Kumbhakonam, 1900, pp. 209.

Translations. A. English. Uttararāmacarita. Translated by Wilson, 1, pp. 275–384.

Uttararāmacarita, a literal translation from the original Sanskrit by H. Mukhopadhyaya. Calcutta, 1871, pp. 84.
Uttararāmacarita. Translated into English by C. H. Tawney. 1° ed., Calcutta, 1871, pp. 81; 2° ed., 1874, pp. 101.
Uttararāmacarita. An English Translation by K. K. Bhattacharya. Calcutta, 1891, pp. 142.

B. French. Le Dénouement de l'histoire de Rama, Outtara Rama Charita, drame de Bhavabhouti, traduit avec une introduction sur la vie et les oeuvres de ce poète par F. Nève. Brussels and Paris, 1880.

C. Hindi. Uttar Ram Carita, by L. Sita Rāma. Allahabad, 1899, pp. 96. Our Ancient Theatre, no. 2.

D. Tamil. Kusulava nātaka by Binadhitten, a translation of the Uttararāmacarita, Cat. Mack. Coll. p. 218.

General Criticism of Bhavabhūti. Borooah, Anundoram. Bhavabhūti and his Place in Sanskrit Literature. Calcutta, 1878, pp. 64.
Banerjea, K. M. Bhavabhūti in English Garb. In IA. 1 (1872), pp. 143–147.
Bhandarkar, R. G. Bhavabhūti's Quotation from the Rāmāyaṇa. In IA. 1 (1873), pp. 123.
Schuyler, Montgomery, Jr. A Bibliography of the Plays of Bhavabhūti and of Kṛṣṇamiśra. In JAOS. 25 (1904), pp. 189–196.

Bhāvanāpuruṣottama *see* **Śrīnivāsātirātrayājin.**

Bhikṣāṭana (?) A 1. p. 412.

Bhīmaṭa Kaliñjarapati wrote five plays (A 1. p. 413), one of which was Svapnadaśānana.

Bhīmavikrama *see* **Mokṣāditya.**

Bhojarājasaccarita *or* Bhojasaccarita *see* **Vedāntavāgīśa.**

Bhūbhaṭṭa Aṅgada A 1. p. 4.

Bilhaṇa, son of Jyeṣṭhakalaśa, (middle of the eleventh century; mentioned in the Rājataraṅgiṇī, 7. 938) Karṇasundarī nāṭikā A 1. p. 82 = 3 Mss.

Idem Karṇasundarī, a drama in four acts. Edited by Durgāprasāda and Parab. Bombay, 1888, pp. 6 + 56. Kāvyamālā, no. 7.

Idem Karṇasundarī, translated into Marathi by V. Śāstri. Bombay, 1891.

Bindumādhava Kampanīpratāpamaṇḍana, a short drama. Poona, 1881–82, pp. 26. In Kāvyetihāsasaṃgraha, 4, no. 12; 5, no. 1.

Bindumatī durmallikā mentioned in SD. 553.

Bṛhannāṭaka, probably the Mahānāṭaka, A 1. p. 376.

Bṛhatsābhadraka prahasana mentioned in RS.

C

Caitanyacandrodaya *see* **Kavikarṇapūra.**

Caṇḍakauśika *see* **Kṣemīśvara.**

Caṇḍīvilāsa *see* **Rudraśarman.**

Candrābhiṣeka A 1. p. 182 = TT. 64.

Candragomin (7th century) Lokānanda L. app. p. 80. There is a Tibetan translation, according to Lévi, app. p. 56.

Candraka, a playwright mentioned in Rājataraṅgiṇī 2. 16.

Candrakalā *see* **Nārāyaṇa Kavi** *and* **Viśvanātha Kavirāja.**

Candrakalāpariṇaya *see* **Nṛsiṃha Kavi.**

Candraprabhā nāṭikā A 1. p. 181 = 3 Mss.; A 2. p. 199.

Candrarekhāvidyādhara A 1. p. 181.

Candraśekhara, father of Viśvanātha, author of the Sāhityadarpaṇa, Puṣpamālā quoted in SD. 282.

Candraśekhara Rāyaguru, son of Gopinātha, Madhurāniruddha, a drama in eight acts, A 1. p. 426; CS. 241. Analyzed by Wilson, 2, pp. 396–399.

Idem Mathurānāṭaka A 1. p. 422, probably the same.

Candraśekharavilāsa *see* **Shahji.**

Candravilāsa *see* **Gaṅgādhara.**

Chalitarāma A 1. p. 192.

Chaṭa Yati (16th century) Vāsantikāpariṇaya A 1. p. 566.

Chāyānāṭaka *see* **Viṭṭhala.**

Citrabhārata *see* **Kṣemendra.**

Citrayajña *see* **Vaidyanātha Vācaspati.**

Cittavṛttikalyāṇa *see* **Nallādīkṣita.**

Cokkanātha, son of Tippa (beginning of 18th century), Kāntimatīpariṇaya A 1. p. 92.

Idem Rasavilāsa bhāṇa A 2. p. 116.

Cola *see* **Varadācārya.**

Cūḍāmaṇināṭaka A 1. p. 189.

Cūḍāmaṇi Sṛṅgārasarvasva bhāṇa quoted in his Kāvyadarpaṇa (cf. A 2. p. 158).

Cūḍāmaṇi Dīkṣita Ānandarāghava (a drama, A 2. p. 189) A 1. p. 48 = 6 Mss.

Idem Kamalinīkalahaṃsa A 1. p. 81 = 12 Mss.; A 2. pp. 15, 191; A 3. p. 18; Hz. 3. 1580.

Idem Rukmiṇīkalyāṇa A 1. p. 527 — 4 Mss. and 2 Com.; A 2. p. 123.

D

Dāḍima Bhaṭṭa Liṅgadurbheda A 1. p. 544 (cf. L. app. p. 80).

Dāmacarita *or* Śrīdāmacarita *see* **Sāmarāja Dīkṣita.**

Ḍamaruka *see* **Ghanaśyāma.**

Dāmodara Kaṃsavadha A 1. p. 77.

Dāmodara Miśra (redactor of the older recension of the Mahānāṭaka of Hanuman) Vāṇībhūṣaṇa. Edited by Śivadatta and Parab. Bombay, 1895, pp. 7 + 53. Kāvyamālā, no. 53.

Dānakeli *see* **Rūpa Gosvāmin.**

Dānakelikaumudī *see* **Mahādeva** *and* **Rūpa Gosvāmin.**

Daṇḍin *see* **Uddaṇḍin.**

Devadurgatī *see* **Rāmmoy.**

Devīmahādeva ullāpya mentioned in SD. 545.

Dhanaṃjayavijaya (?) SCBen. 266.

Dhanaṃjayavijaya *see* **Kāñcanācārya** *and* **Yaśodhana.**

Dharmagupta, son of Rāmadāsa, wrote in 1360, Rāmāṅka nāṭikā A 1. p. 268.

Dharma Paṇḍita *or* **Dharmasūri,** son of Parvateśvara, Narakāsuravijaya vyāyoga (also called Narakāsuravadha, Narakāsuradhvaṃsa, or Narakadhvaṃsa) A 1. p. 277 = 8 Mss.; A 2. p. 60 = 5 Mss; IO. 7. 4185.

Idem Narakāsuravijaya vyāyoga. 2° ed., Madras, 1884, pp. 166.

Dharmarāja Sabhāpativilāsa A 1. p. 696.

Dharmavijaya *see* **Śukla Bhūdeva.**

Dhūrta (= Dhūrtasamāgama) *see* **Jyotirīśvara.**

Dhūrtacarita prahasana mentioned in SD. 536.

Dhūrtanartaka *see* **Sāmarāja.**

Dhūrtasamāgama *see* **Jyotirīśvara.**

Dhūrtaviḍambana *see* **Maheśvara.**

Ḍiṇḍima Kavi Somavallīyogānanda prahasana A 1. p. 736 = 2 Mss.

Idem Somavallīyogānanda. Edited by S. P. V. Ranganadhasvami Ayyavaralugaru. Vizagapatam, 1895. Grandha Pradarśani, fasc. 1–2.

Draupadīpariṇaya *see* **Kṛṣṇa Sūri.**

Dṛgbhavat Nīlāpariṇaya A 1. p. 302 (cf. L. app. p. 76).

Dūtāṅgada *see* **Subhaṭa.**

G

Gairvanivijaya *see* **Bāla Kavi.**

Gaṅgādhara (14th century) Candravilāsa A 2. p. 36.

Idem Gaṅgādāsapratāpavilāsa *or* Pratāpavilāsa IO. 7. 4194 (Analyzed).

Idem Rāghavābhyudaya A 1. p. 500 = 2 Mss.

Gaṅgāvataraṇa A 3. p. 30.

Gaurīdigambara *see* **Śaṅkara Miśra.**

Ghanaśyāma, son of Mahādeva, (cf. E. Hultzsch, in Hz. 3. pp. ix–xi) Ānandasundarī saṭṭaka Hz. 3. 2142.

Idem Ḍamaruka. Com. by Candraśekhara, son of Ghanaśyāma, Hz. 3. 1674.

Idem Kumāravijaya A 3. p 38; Hz. 3. 1682.

Idem Madanasaṃjīvana Hz. 3. 1679.

Idem Navagrahacarita Hz. 3. 1571.

Idem Pracaṇḍarāhūdaya. Com., Hz. 3. 1675.

Girvānendra, son of Nīlakaṇṭha Dīkṣita, Śṛṅgārakośa bhāṇa, mentioned in preface to Patañjalicarita in Kāvyamālā, no. 51, p. 22.

Gītadigambara *see* **Vaṃśamaṇi.**

Godāpariṇaya *see* **Keśavanātha.**

Godāvarīpariṇaya A 1. p. 159. Probably the same as the Godāpariṇaya.

Gokulanātha Amṛtodaya A 1. p. 29; A 3. p. 7.

Idem Amṛtodaya nāṭaka, edited by Śivadatta and Parab. Bombay, 1897, pp. 5 + 73. Kāvyamālā, no. 59.

Idem Madālasā A 2. p. 97 = 1 Ms. and 1 Com.

Gopāla Bhaṭṭa Sānandagovinda A 1. p. 707 (cf. L. app. p. 81).

Gopāladāsa Pārijātaharaṇa A 1. p. 335 = 2 Mss.

Gopālalīlārṇava *see* **Govinda.**

Gopālarāya Śrīraṅgarāja bhāṇa A 2. p. 160 = 2 Mss.

Idem Śṛṅgāramañjarī bhāṇa A 2. p. 158.

Gopīcandana A 1. p. 163.

Gopīnātha Paṇḍita Kautukasarvasva prahasana A 1. p. 131 = TT. 63; A 3. p. 28. Analyzed by Wilson, 2, pp. 410–412, and by Cappeller in Gurupūjākaumudī, Festgabe für Weber, Leipzig, 1896, pp. 59–62.

Goṣayātrā *see* **Ṣitalacandra.**

Govardhana, a playwright, DR. intr. p. 30 n.

Govinda Gopālalīlārṇava bhāṇa A 1. p. 163.

Idem Vinatānanda vyāyoga A 1. p. 576.

Govinda Kavibhūṣaṇa Samṛddhamādhava A 3. p. 36.

Govindavallabha A 1. p. 169.

Gundarāma Miśrabhāṇa L. app. p. 78.

Gururāmakavi Subhadrādhanaṃjaya A 1. p. 728 = 9 Mss.

H

Hanuman.

Mahānāṭaka. This play exists in two recensions, an older one by Dāmodara, explained by Mohanadāsa, and a more recent one by Madhusūdana.

Manuscripts. A 1. p. 438 = 54 Mss. and 2 Com.; by Candraśekhara 1, by Nārāyaṇa 1, by Balabhadra 4, by Mohanadāsa 11; A 2. pp. 100, 216 = 7 Mss. and Com. by Balabhadra 1, by Mohanadāsa 4; CBMMS. 264, 265; IO. 7. 4145, 4146, 4147, 4148, 4149, 4150; TT. 59; Com. by Mohanadāsa, IO. 7. 4149; Com. by Candraśekhara, IO. 7. 4150. There was a Ms. in the possession of Sir Monier Williams. Analyzed by Wilson, 2, pp. 363–373.

Sītāsvayaṃvara from the Mahānāṭaka A 1. p. 723.

Text Editions. Mahānāṭaka. [An edition in Bengali characters, published before 1840. For the editor cf. JA. 3° series, 13 (1842), p. 510, and Gildemeister, Bibl. Sans., p. 95.]

Mahānāṭaka. A dramatic history of King Rāma. Translated into English and edited by K. K. Bahadur. Calcutta, 1840, 2 pts., pp. 108 + 117.

Mahānāṭaka. Drama on the deeds of Rāma ascribed to Hanuman. Edited in the Bengali version by Iśvaracandra and Kālīnātha. Calcutta, 1844, pp. 229.

Hanuman-Nāṭaka in Dāmodara's recension. With Mohanadāsa's commentary. 1° ed., Bombay, 1860, pp. 107; 2° ed., 1886, pp. 241.

Hanuman Nāṭaka. The story of the Rāmāyaṇa dramatized in Dāmodara's version and divided into 14 acts. With Mohanadāsa's commentary. 1° ed., Bombay, 1863, pp. 122; 2° ed., 1864, pp. 93.

Mahānāṭaka by Hanuman, edited by R. Śiromaṇi with a short commentary of his own. Calcutta, 1870, pp. 2 + 176.

Mahānāṭaka in 9 acts. Compiled by Madhusūdana. Edited by J. Vidyāsāgara. 1° ed., Calcutta, 1878, pp. 127; 2° ed., 1890, pp. 450.

Mahānāṭaka, with a commentary by Miśra Mohana. Bombay, 1886, pp. 241.

Translations. Mahanatak. In Sanskrit and Bengali, dramatized (?) by Ramgāti Kabiratna. 1° ed., Calcutta, 1849; 2° ed., 1851, pp. 229.

Mahānāṭaka. Translated into English by Raja Kali Krishna. Calcutta, no date.

Hanuman nāṭaka, translated into Hindustani. Lahore, 1877, pp. 192.

Haracāpāropaṇa A 1. p. 754.

Haragaurīvivāha *see* **Jagajjyotirmalla.**

Harakeli *see* **Vigraharājadeva.**

Hari (Ācārya) Jānakīgītā A 3. p. 44.

Haridāsa Harivilāsa bhāṇa A 2. p. 183.

Idem Purañjana A 1. p. 339.

Haridūta chāyānāṭaka A 1. p. 757. Analyzed by Lévi, p. 242.

Harihara, a Maithila, Bhartṛharinirveda A 1. p. 397.

Idem Bhartṛharinirveda. Edited by Durgāprasāda and Parab. 1° ed., Bombay, 1892, pp. 3 + 28 ; 2° ed., 1900. Kāvyamālā, no. 29.

Idem The Bhartṛharinirveda of Harihara, now first translated from the Sanskrit and Prākrit by Louis H. Gray. In JAOS. 25 (1904), pp. 197–230.

Idem Bhartṛharinirveda. Analyzed in The Nīti and Vairāgya Śatakas of Bhartṛhari, by Gopi Nath, Bombay, 1896, pp. 19–24.

Idem Prabhāvatīpariṇaya A 1. p. 354.

Hariharānusaraṇayātrā *see* **Nṛsiṃha Bhaṭṭa.**

Harijīvana Miśra Vijayapārijāta A 1. p. 570.

Hariścandrayaśaścandracandrikā A 1. p. 761.

Harivilāsa *see* **Haridāsa.**

Harṣadeva.

Nāgānanda nāṭaka. *Manuscripts.* A 1. p. 283 = 16 Mss. and 1 Com.; by Ātmārāma 1 ; A 2. p. 61 = 3 Mss ; A 3. p. 61 = 3 Mss. ; Hz. 3. 1610 ; IO. 7. 4161. Cf. also the preface to Boyd's edition of the Nāgānanda.

Text Editions. Nāgānanda. A Sanskrit Drama by Dhāvaka. Calcutta, 1864.

Nāgānanda, a Sanskrit drama in five acts. Edited by M. Ghosha and K. Bhaṭṭācārya. Calcutta, 1864, pp. 74 + 19.

Nāgānanda, with a Marathi translation. Edited with a preface in Marathi by K. S. Chipaḷūṇakar. Bombay, 1865, pp. 2 + 206.

Nāgānanda. Edited by J. Vidyāsāgara. 1° ed., Calcutta, 1873; 2° ed., 1886, pp. 138.

Nāgānanda. Edited with a commentary by N. C. Kaviratna and N. C. Śiromaṇi. Calcutta, 1886.

Nāgānanda. Text with notes by Pandit N. C. Vidyaratna and with translations into English and Bengali by a Professor of the Presidency College. Calcutta, 1887, pp. 324.

Nāgānanda, a Sanskrit Drama by King Śrī-Harsha. Edited with copious Sanskrit and English notes by S. G. Bhānap. Bombay, 1892, pp. 18 + 91 + 40.

Nāgānanda, edited with an introduction and notes by G. B. Brahme and S. M. Paranjape. Poona, 1893, pp. 27 + 105 + 80.

Translations. A. English. Nāgānanda, or the Joy of the Snake World, a Buddhist Drama in Five Acts. Translated into English Prose, with explanatory notes, from the Sanskrit of Śrī-Harsha-Deva by Palmer Boyd. With an Introduction by Professor Cowell. London, 1872, pp. 14 + 99.

B. French. Nāgānanda. La Joie des Serpents, drame bouddhique traduit du Sanskrit et du Prākrit par Abel Bergaigne. Paris, 1879, pp. 16 + 44. Bibl. Orient. Elzévir., no. 27.

C. Italian. Amori di Indiani. L'atto secondo del drama di Dhāvaka che è detto Nāgānanda o la Allegria de' serpenti. Da Emilio Teza. Pisa, pp. 16.

Nāgānanda, o il Giubilo dei Serpenti. Traduzione di Francesco Cimmino. Palermo, 1903, pp. 63 + 167.

Criticism. Beal, S. The Nāgānanda, a Buddhist drama. In The Academy, Sept. 29, 1883, vol. 24, pp. 217–218.

Cimmino, Francesco. Sul Dramma Nāgānanda, o il Giubilo dei Serpenti. In Atti della Reale Accademia di Archeologia, Lettere e Belle Arti (di Napoli), 22 (1902), pp. 155–182.

Cimmino, Francesco. Une communication sur le drame Nāgānanda. In Verh. des 13. intern. Orientalisten-Kongr. (1902), Leiden, 1904, pp. 31–32.

Priyadarśikā nāṭikā. *Manuscripts.* A 1. p. 364 = 11 Mss.; A 3. p. 78; Hz. 3. 1609.

Text Editions. Priyadarśika. Without place or date (about 1870), pp. 56.

Priyadarśikā. A drama in four acts by Śrī Harsha. Edited with notes by J. Vidyāsāgara. Calcutta, 1874, pp. 61.

Priyadarśikā. Edited by V. D. Gadre with English notes and Prākrita Chāyā. Bombay, 1884, pp. 94.

Translation. Priyadarśikā, pièce en quatre actes, traduite par G. Strehly. Précédée d'un prologue et d'une introduction. Paris, 1888, pp. 88. Bibl. Orient. Elzévir., no. 58.

Criticism. Cimmino, Francesco. Il terzo atto del dramma indiano Priyadarçikā. In Atti dell' Accademia Pontaniana, 31 (1902), pp. 1–18.

Ratnāvalī nāṭikā. *Manuscripts.* A 1. p. 492 = 37 Mss. and 1 Com.; by Bhīmasena 2, translation of the Prākrit passages by Mudgaladeva 1; A 2. p. 115 = 8 Mss. and Com. by Govinda 2, Prākṛtachāyā 2; CBMMS. 275; CS. 257; Hz. 3. 1608; IO. 7. 4159, 4160; TT. 65; Com., SCBen. 290.

Text Editions. Ratnāvalī. With a commentary explanatory of the Prākrit passages. Calcutta, 1832, pp. 106.

Ratnāvalī. Edited with a translation of the Prākrit passages into Sanskrit by Tārānātha Śarman. Calcutta, 1864, pp. 66.

Ratnāvalī. By Śrīharṣadeva. Text. Bombay, 1868, pp. 74.

Ratnāvalī. Edited by N. C. M. Vidyaratna. With notes explanatory of the difficult passages. Calcutta, 1871, pp. 4 + 122.

Ratnāvalī, edited with a commentary by J. Vidyāsāgara. Calcutta, 1876, pp. 124.

Ratnāvalī, herausgegeben von C. Cappeller, in O. von Böhtlingk, Sanskrit Chrestomathie, St. Petersburg, 1877, pp. 290–329.

Ratnāvalī, edited with notes by N. B. Godabole and K. P. Parab. 1° ed., Bombay, 1882, pp. 102; 2° ed., 1890, pp. 112.

Ratnāvalī, edited by K. P. Parab and V. S. Jośī. Bombay, 1888, pp. 81.

Ratnāvalī, published with Siddhanta Bindu by V. S. Aiyar. Kumbhakonam, 1893, pp. 212. Advaitamañjarī Series, no. 3.

Ratnāvalī, with the commentary of Govinda, edited by K. P. Parab. Bombay, 1895.

Ratnāvalī. Text with a commentary by K. N. Nyāyapañcānana. Calcutta, 1900, pp. 198.

Ratnavoli, edited by Sris Chandra Chakravarti. Containing the text, a Sanskrit commentary, English and Bengali translations, etc. Dacca (Bengal), 1902, pp. 387.

Translations. A. English. Ratnāvalī, or the Necklace. Translated by Wilson, 2, pp. 255–319.

B. German. Ratnavali, oder die Perlenschnur, zum ersten Male ins Deutsche übersetzt von Ludwig Fritze. Chemnitz, 1878. In his Indisches Theater, vol. 2.

C. Swedish. Ratnavali, eller Pärlbandet. Från Sanskrit öfversatt af H. Andersson. Wexiö, 1892, pp. 76.

D. Italian. Ratnāvalī, o la Collana di Perle, dramma indiano, tradotto per la prima volta in italiano da Francesco Cimmino. Naples, 1894, pp. 199.

E. Bengali. Ratnabali. Translated from the Sanskrit into Bengali by Nilmani Pal. Calcutta, no date.

F. Marathi. Lalitawatsaraj, a Marathi translation of the Ratnavali of Çriharsadeva, by V. S. Islampurkar. Bombay, 1889, pp. 115 + 109.

G. Canarese. Rathnavali, a tale in Canarese founded on Sriharsa Dava's [sic] Sanskrit drama. Bangalore, 1884, pp. 44.

Criticism. Bühler, Georg. On the Authorship of the Ratnāvalī. In IA. 2 (1873), pp. 127–128.

Hall, F. [References to the Ratnāvạlī.] In the preface to his Vāsavadattā, Calcutta, 1859, pp. 15–18.

Meyer, J. J. Dāmodaragupta's Kuṭṭanīmatam (Lehren einer Kupplerin). Leipzig, 1903, pp. 143–144. [Description of the performance of part of the first act of the Ratnāvalī. The text was printed in Kāvyamālā, part 3 (1887), pp. 32–111].

Vidyabhusan, S. C. Date of the Ratnāvalī. In Maha-Bodhi, 12.

General Criticism of Harṣadeva. Beames, John. Chand's mention of Śrī Harsha. In IA. 2 (1873), p. 240.

Jackson, A. V. Williams. Time Analysis of Sanskrit Plays. Second Series. The Dramas of Harsha. In JAOS. 21 (1900), pp. 88–108.

Pischel, R. Āḍhyarāja. In Nachr. der Kōnig. Ges. der Wiss. zu Göttingen, Philol.-Hist. Klasse, 1901, pp. 485–487.

Rām Dās Sen. Chand's mention of Śrī Harsha. In IA. 2 (1873), p. 240, and 3 (1874), p. 31.

Schuyler, Montgomery, Jr. The Origin of the Vidūṣaka, and the employment of this character in the plays of Harṣadeva. In JAOS. 20 (1899), pp. 338–340.

Schuyler, Montgomery, Jr. A Bibliography of the Plays attributed to Harṣadeva. In Verh. des 13. intern. Orientalisten-Kongr. (1902), Leiden, 1904, pp. 33–37.

Telang, K. T. Kālidāsa, Śrī Harsha, and Chand. In IA. 3 (1874), pp. 81–83.

Telang, K. T. Kālidāsa and Śrī Harsha. In IA. 4 (1875), pp. 84–85.

Harṣanātha Śarman Uṣāharaṇa. A modern copy in the hands of Mr. Grierson.

Hastimalla, a Jain, Añjanāpavanaṃjaya L. app. p. 73.

Hastimallasena, a Jain, Arjunarāja A 1. p. 30.

Idem Bharataraja A 1. p. 396.

Idem Maithilīpariṇaya A 1. p. 468.

Idem Megheśvara A 1. p. 466.

Hāsyacūḍāmaṇi *see* **Vatsarāja.**

Hāsyaratnākara mentioned in DR. intr. p. 30.

Hāsyārṇava *see* **Jagadīśvara.**

Hṛdayavinoda *see* **Kavi Paṇḍita.**

I

Indirāpariṇaya A 1. p. 58.

Indirāpariṇaya *see* **Vīrarāghava.**

Indumatīpariṇaya A 1. p. 59.

J

Jagadīśvara Hāsyārṇava prahasana A 1. p. 766 = 9 Mss. and Com. by Mahendranātha 1; A 2. p. 237; A 3. p. 158; IO. 7. 4191, 4192, 4193 (with an English translation); TT. 62. Analyzed by Wilson, 2, pp. 408–409.

Idem Hāsyārṇava. [An edition published in 1835; cf. Aufrecht, Cat. Codd. Sanscr. Bibl. Bodl., Oxford, 1864.]

Idem Hāsyārṇava. The verse of the original Sanskrit comedy with a Bengali translation of the whole work. Calcutta, 1840, pp. 116.

Idem Hāsyārṇava, ed. C. Cappeller. [Jena, 1883], pp. 28. [Autographed.]

Jagajjyotirmalla (wrote in 1629) Haragaurīvivāha L. app. p. 82.

Jaganmohana L. app. p. 75.

Jagannātha, son of Pītāmbara, Atandracandrika A 1. p. 6 = 2 Mss.; A 2. pp. 2, 186.

Jagannātha Paṇḍita Anaṅgavijaya bhāṇa A 1. p. 12; Hz. 3. 1776.

Idem Ratimanmatha Hz. 3. 1604.

Idem Vasumatīpariṇaya A 1. p. 557.

Jagannāthavallabha *see* **Rāmānanda.**

Jaitrajaivātṛka *see* **Nārāyaṇa Śāstrin.**

Jāmadagnyajaya, a vyāyoga or subject of a vyāyoga mentioned in DR. 3. 55.

Jāmbavatīkalyāṇa *see* **Kṛṣṇarāya.**

Jānakīgītā *see* **Hari.**

Jānakīpariṇaya A 1. p. 206 = 2 Mss.

Jānakīpariṇaya *see* **Nārāyaṇa Bhaṭṭa, Rāmabhadra Dīkṣita,** *and* **Sītārāma.**

Jānakīrāghava quoted in SD. 371, and by Rāmanātha in his Trikāṇḍaviveka.

Jātavedas Pūrṇapuruṣārthacandra A 1. p. 343; A 2. p. 76.

Jayadeva, son of Mahādeva.

Prasannarāghava. *Manuscripts.* A 1. p. 359 = 46 Mss. and 1 Com.; A 2. pp. 81, 211 = 7 Mss. and Com. by Raghunandana 1; CS. 237, 238; Hz. 3. 1576; IO. 7. 4158.

Text Editions. The Prasannarāghava. Edited by G. D. Śāstri. Benares, 1868, pp. 165.

Prasannarāghava. Edited by J. Vidyāsāgara. Calcutta, 1872, pp. 168.

Prasannarāghava. Edited by R. S. Vavilla. 1° ed., Madras, 1874, pp. 126; 2° ed., 1882, pp. 82; 3° ed., 1890, pp. 82.

Prasannarāghava. Edited by K. P. Parab. Bombay, 1893, pp. 146.

Prasannarāghava. Edited with introduction and notes by S. R. Khopakar, with the commentary of Vyankatācārya. Bombay, 1894, pp. 412.

Prasannarāghava. Edited with introduction and notes by S. M. Paranjape and N. S. Panse. Poona, 1894, 2 pts., pp. 209 + 106.

Jayanta Bhaṭṭa Ṣaṇmata A 3. p. 43.

Jīvānanda A 1. p. 208.

Jīvānanda Jyotirvid Maṅgalanāṭaka, an original mythological play in nine acts, on the greatness of Devī, in Sanskrit and Hindi. Benares, 1887, pp. 137.

Jīvānandana *see* **Ānandarāya.**

Jīvanmuktikalyāṇa *see* **Mallāsomayājin** *and* **Nallādīkṣita.**

Jīvarāma Yājñika Murārivijaya CS. 250.

Jīvavibudha (before the second half of the seventeenth century) Nalānanda A 1. p. 280.

Jñānasūryodaya *see* **Vādicandra.**

Jyotirīśvara Kaviśekhara,

son of Dhīreśvara, (second half of fifteenth century).

Dhūrtasamāgama prahasana A 1. p. 272 = 8 Mss.; A 2. pp.

59 = 2 Mss.; SCBen. 288; IO. 7. 4201. Analyzed by Wilson, 2, p. 408.

Text Editions. Dhūrtasamāgama, herausgegeben von Carl Cappeller. [Jena, 1883], pp. 16. [Autographed.]

Dhūrtasamāgama, comoedia e cod. Parisiensi Sanskrite cum annotationibus edidit Chr. Lassen. In Anthologia Sanscritica, Bonn, 1838, pp. 68–96, 116–130.

Translations. A. French. Dhūrtasamāgama, pièce de théâtre hindou, traduite du Sanscrit par Ch. Schoebel. Without place or date, pp. 24.

B. Italian. Dhūrtasamāgama, ossia il congresso de' bricconi. Farsa di Giotirisvaro. In Teatro scelto indiano tradotto dal Sanscrito da Antonio Marazzi, vol. 2, Milan, 1874, pp. 189–231. [Published originally in the Giornale Napolitano di Filosofia e Lettere, Aug.–Sept., 1872.]

K

Kādamba Rāmakṛṣṇa Aditikuṇḍalāharaṇa A 2. p. 2 = 2 Mss.

Kādambarīrāma, a playwright, A 1. p. 92.

Kalānanda *see* **Rāmacandra Kavi.**

Kalāvatīkāmarūpa A 1. p. 84.

Kāleyakutūhala *see* **Bharadvāja.**

Kālidāsa.

Mālavikāgnimitra. *Manuscripts.* A 1. pp. 453–454 = 40 Mss. and 3 Com.; by Kāṭayavema 2, by Vīrarāghava 1; A 2. pp. 104, 217 = 4 Mss. and Com. by Kāṭayavema 2, by Nīlakaṇṭha 2; A 3. p. 98 = 3 Mss.; CS. 245, 246; Hz. 3. 1574; IO. 7. 4122; TT. 67. Analyzed by Wilson, 2, p. 345.

Text Editions. Mālavikāgnimitra. Textum primus edidit et varietatem scripturae adjecit O. F. Tullberg. Vol. 1, Bonn, 1840, pp. 9 + 108.

Mālavikāgnimitra. Bombay, 1868, pp. 4 + 89.

Mālavikāgnimitra. Edited with notes by S. P. Pandit. 1° ed.,

Bombay, 1869, pp. 39 + 164; 2° ed., with the commentary of Kāṭayavema, 1889, pp. 35 + 230. Bombay Sanskrit Series, no. 6.

Mālavikāgnimitra. Edited with Notes by T. Tarkavācaspati. 1° ed., Calcutta, 1870, pp. 165. 2° ed., 1887, pp. 148.

Mālavikāgnimitra. Mit kritischen und erklärenden Anmerkungen herausgegeben von F. Bollensen. Leipzig, 1879.

Mālavikāgnimitra, with the commentary named Kumāragirirājīya of Kāṭayavema. Vizagapatam, 1884, pp. 133.

Mālavikāgnimitra. Edited with an original commentary by Mrityuñjaya Niṣṣanka. Madras, 1885, pp. 262.

Mālavikāgnimitra. Little Conjevaram, 1886, pp. 64.

Mālavikāgnimitra. Sanskrit text with full notes in English by M. C. Sadagopachariar. Bombay, 1889.

Mālavikāgnimitra, edited with the commentary of Kāṭayavema and with explanatory English notes by K. P. Parab. Bombay, 1890, pp. 153.

Mālavikāgnimitra. Edited with the commentary of Kāṭayavema. Bombay, 1891, pp. 112.

Mālavikāgnimitra. With the commentary of Kāṭayavema. Edited with explanatory English notes. Bombay, 1891, pp. 158.

Mālavikāgnimitra, with the commentary of Kāṭayavema and several others embodied therein, edited with critical notes and translation by S. S. Ayyar. Poona, 1896, pp. 303.

Mālavikāgnimitra, edited with a close English translation by S. B. Bhāgvat. Poona, 1897, pp. 126.

Mālavikāgnimitra. Edited with a commentary, notes, and translation by M. C. Śatakopācāri. Kumbhakonam, 1900, pp. 152.

Translations. A. English. Mālavikāgnimitra, translated into English prose by C. H. Tawney. 1° ed., Calcutta, 1875, pp. 93; 2° ed., 1891, pp. 121.

Mālavikāgnimitra, translated into English prose by G. R. Nandargikar. Poona, 1879, pp. 53.

B. French. Malavika et Agnimitra. Traduit pour la première

fois en français par P. E. Foucaux. Paris, 1877, pp. 11 + 118. Bibl. Orient. Elzévir., no. 14.

Mālavikāgnimitra. Agnimitra et Mālavikā, comédie en cinq actes et un prologue, mêlée de prose et de vers, traduite du sanscrit et du prâcrit par Victor Henry. Paris, 1889, pp. 12 + 110. (Extr. des Mém. de la Soc. des Sciences de Lille.)

C. German. Mālavikā und Agnimitra, ein Drama des Kālidāsa in fünf Akten, zum ersten Male übersetzt von Albrecht Weber. Berlin, 1856, pp. 48 + 107.

Malavika und Agnimitra, metrisch übersetzt von Ludwig Fritze. Leipzig, 1881, pp. 74.

Mālavikāgnimitra. Prinzessin Zofe. Ein indisches Lustspiel in vier Aufzügen nebst einem Vorspiel, frei für die deutsche Bühne bearbeitet von Leopold von Schroeder. Munich, 1902, pp. 8 + 70.

D. Dutch. Danseres en Koning. Malavika en Agnimitra. Tooneelstuk uit het Sanskret vertaald door J. van der Vliet. Haarlem, 1882, pp. 132.

E. Swedish. Mālavikā. Ett indiskt skådespel. Från Sanskrit öfversatt af H. Edgren. Malmö, 1877.

F. Danish. Kongen og Danserinden. Lystspil i fem Akter. Oversat af E. Brandes. Med tegninger af C. Thomsen. Copenhagen, 1874.

G. Italian. Malavica ed Agnimitro. Dramma in cinque atti. In Teatro scelto indiano, tradotto dal Sanscrito da Antonio Marazzi, vol. 1, Milan, 1871, pp. 301–417.

Mālavikāgnimitra. Dramma indiano tradotto in italiano da Francesco Cimmino. Naples, 1897, pp. 11 + 126.

H. Bohemian. Mālavikā a Agnimitra. Preložil Zubatý. Prague, 1893, pp. 102. Sbornik světové poesie, no. 16.

I. Bengali. Mālavikāgnimitra, translated in Bengali by S. M. Tagore. Calcutta, 1877.

J. Marathi. Rāja Agnimitra, a Marathi translation of the Mālavikāgnimitra by V. S. Islampurkar. Bombay, 1889, pp. 204.

Mālavikāgnimitra. Translated into Marathi by Rāo S. N. G. Rāje. Bombay, 1895, pp. 156.

Sangīta Mālavikāgnimitra Nātak, or the drama of Mālavikā and Agnimitra in musical verse. Translated into Marathi by B. G. Varde. Bombay, 1895, pp. 136.

K. Hindi. Mālavikāgnimitra. Translated from Sanskrit into Hindi by Sīta Rāma. Cawnpore, 1899, pp. 70.

L. Gujarati. Mālavikāgnimitra. Translated into Gujarati by R. Udayarama. Bombay, 1870, pp. 109.

Criticism. Annotations on Sanskrit Classics. The Mālavikāgnimitra. In The Sanskrit Reader (Saṃskṛtapāṭhāvalī), Bombay, 1884, vol. 2, pt. 4, pp. 48.

Bollensen, Friedrich. Beiträge zur Erklärung der Mālavikā. In ZDMG. 13 (1859), pp. 480-490.

Cappeller, Carl. Observationes ad Kālidāsae Mālavikāgnimitram. Königsberg, no date, pp. 33.

Cimmino, Francesco. Alcune osservazioni sul dramma Mālavikāgnimitra. In Atti dell' Accademia Pontaniana, 33 (1904), pp. 1-16.

Haag, Friedrich. Zur Texteskritik und Erklärung von Kālidāsa's Mālavikāgnimitra. Erster Teil. Auszug aus dem Progr. der Kantonsschule pro 1871-72. Frauenfeld, 1872.

Schuyler, Montgomery, Jr. Bibliography of Kālidāsa's Mālavikāgnimitra and Vikramorvaśī. In JAOS. 23 (1902), pp. 93-101.

Vliet, J. van der. Mālavikā-Mañjulikā. In Bijdrage voor de taal- land- en volkenkunde van Nederlandsch Indie, 6. vol greeks, 5 (= 49), p. 169-170.) [On resemblances between the Mālavikāgnimitra and the Kathāsaritsāgara.]

Weber, Albrecht. Zur Erklärung der Mālavikā. In ZDMG. 14 (1860), p. 261.

Śakuntalā. *Manuscripts.* A 1. p. 23 = 88 Mss. and 4 Com.; by Abhirāma 2, by Kāṭayavema 6, by Kṛṣṇanātha Pañcānana 1, by Candraśekhara 2, by Ḍamaruvallabha 1, by Nārāyaṇa 3, by Rāghava 4, by Rāmabhadra 1, by Śaṅkara 1, by Śrīnivāsa 2; A 2. p. 5 = 6 Mss. and 3 Com.; by Candraśekhara 1, by Rāghava 2; A 2. p. 187 = 4 Mss. and 4 Com.; by Rāghava 1, by Vemabhūpāla; A 3. p. 6 = 16

Mss. and 1 Com.; by Abhirāma 2, by Kāṭayavema 2, by Rāghava 2, by Śrīnivāsa 4, Prākṛtachāyā 2; CBMMS. 263; Hz. 3. 1756; IO. 7. 4110, 4111, 4112, 4113, 4114, 4115, 4116; TT. 60; Com. by Nārāyaṇa, SCBen. 295; Com. by Candraśekhara, IO. 7. 4117, 4118; Com. by Ghanaśyāma, Hz. 3. 1656; Com., SCBen. 981, IO. 7. 4119.

Text Editions. Śakuntalā. Calcutta, 1761. [First printed edition.]

La Reconoissance de Sacountala, drame sanscrit et prakrit de Calidasa, publié sur un manuscript unique de la Bibliothèque du Roi, accompagné d'une traduction française, de notes philologiques, critiques et littéraires, par A. L. Chézy. 1° ed., Paris, 1830. 2° ed., 1832.

Abhijñānaśakuntalā. With the commentary of Premacandra. Calcutta, 1839, pp. 159. [In Bengali characters.]

Śakuntalā. Neue Ausgabe in lateinischen Typen. (?)

Abhijñānaśakuntalā. Gauriya recension. Edited by P. C. Tarkavāgīśa. 1° ed., Calcutta, 1839, pp. 159; 2° ed., 1860, pp. 170. Reprinted with additional notes by R. S. Tarkaratna, Calcutta, 1864, pp. 190.

Kālidāsa's Ring-Çakuntalā. Herausgegeben, übersetzt und mit Anmerkungen versehen von O. Böhtlingk. Bonn, 1842, large ed.; 1846, small ed. [Devanāgarī recension.]

Śakuntalā Recognized by the Ring, a Sanskrit drama in seven acts. The Devanāgarī recension of the text, with literal English translations of all the metrical passages and notes by M. Williams. 1° ed., Hertford, 1853; 2° ed., Oxford, 1876.

Abhijñānaśakuntalā. Bombay, 1861.

Abhijñāna Śakuntalam. Edited with notes by J. Tarkālaṃkāra and K. Tarkaratna and with a preface in Bengali by V. Majumdār. Calcutta, 1869, pp. 232. In Majumdār's Series.

Śakuntalā. Edited by Jaganmohana Śarman and Kedāranātha. Calcutta, 1869.

Abhijñāna Śakuntalā. Edited with a commentary by D. V. Panta. Calcutta, 1871, pp. 2 + 236.

Sacuntala annulo recognita, fabula scenica Cālidāsi. Textum recensionis devanagaricae recognovit atque glossario sanscritico et pracritico instruxit Carolus Burkhard. Breslau, 1872, pp. 12 + 112 + 227.

Abhijñānaśakuntalā, with Śrīnivāsācārya's commentary, called Śakuntalāvayākhya. Edited by S. Tiruveṅkaṭācārya and V. Rāmakṛṣṇamācārya. Madras, 1874, pp. 6 + 320.

Śakuntalā. The Bengali Recension. With critical notes. Edited by R. Pischel. 1° ed., Kiel, 1877, pp. 11 + 210; 2° ed., 1886, pp. 11 + 210.

Abhijñānaśakuntalā. Edited with notes and explanations by Iśvaracandra Vidyāsāgara. 1° ed., Calcutta, 1880, pp. 262; 2° ed., 1887, pp. 293; 3° ed., 1889, pp. 256.

Śakuntalā, with a commentary by Śrīnivāsācārya. Madras, 1880, pp. 6 + 326.

Śakuntalā. With the commentary of Srīnivāsa Chārlu. Madras, 1882, pp. 320.

Abhijñānaśakuntalā, with the commentary of Rāghavabhaṭṭa. Edited with English notes by N. B. Godabole and K. P. Parab. 1° ed., Bombay, 1883, pp. 331; 2° ed., 1889 (?); 3° ed., 1891, pp. 374.

Abhijñāna-Śakuntalā, with the commentary of Rāghavabhaṭṭa. Edited by N. B. Godabole and K. P. Parab. 1° ed., Bombay, 1883, pp. 167; 2° ed., 1886, pp. 267; 3° ed., 1895, pp. 267.

Śakuntalā, with a commentary by P. Venkatacharia. Madras, 1883, pp. 345.

Śakuntalā. Edited with notes and full explanations by K. N. Nyāyapañcānana. 1° ed., Calcutta, no date, pp. 335; 2° ed., 1888, pp. 2 + 337.

Abhijñānaśakuntalā. Bombay, no date, pp. 50.

Śakuntalānāṭaka. Bombay, no date, pp. 98.

Abhijñānaśakuntalā. Edited with a close English translation and various readings by P. N. Patankar. 1° ed., Poona, 1889, pp. 473; 2° ed., 1902, pp. 358.

Abhijñānaśakuntalam. In Bengali, English, and Sanskrit.

Edited by B. B. Gosvāmi. With notes and English and Bengali translations. Calcutta, 1895, pp. 464.

Abhijñānaśakuntalā. With the commentary of Rāghavabhaṭṭa. Edited with an English translation, notes, and various readings by M. R. Kale. 1° ed., Bombay, 1898, pp. 397; 2° ed., 1902, pp. 397.

Abhijñanaśakuntalā, with an introduction, glossary, English and Bengali translations and various readings. Edited by N. C. Vidyāratna. Calcutta, 1901, pp. 770.

Abhijñānaśakuntalā. Acts 1–5. Text, commentary, introduction, notes, and translation by T. E. Śrīnivāsācāriar and B. S. K. Aiyar. Kumbhakonam, 1901, pp. 178 + 135.

Śakuntalā, or the Fatal Ring; a drama by Kālidāsa, to which is added Meghadūta, and Bhagavadgīta. Edited with an introduction by T. Holme. London, 1902, pp. 240.

Translations. A. English. Śacountalā, or the Fatal Ring, translated from the original Sanskrit and Prakrit [by Sir William Jones]. 1° ed., Calcutta, 1789, pp. 184; 2° ed., London, 1790; 3° ed., London, 1792; 4° ed., Edinburgh, 1796, pp. 161. Reprinted at Calcutta, 1855; London, 1870; Calcutta, 1887, 1899, pp. 74.

Śakuntala, or the Lost Ring. Translated by M. Williams. 1° ed., Hertford, 1853; 2° ed., 1855; 3° ed., 1856; 4° ed., London, 1872; 5° ed., 1887; 6° ed., 1890.

Śakuntala, translated by Monier Williams, edited by B. V. N. Kīrtikar. Bombay, 1885, pp. 98. [An abridgment of Williams's version.]

Śakoontala, or the Lost Ring. Translated by Monier Williams. New York, 1885.

Śakuntalā. An English translation by Kṛṣṇa Kamal Bhaṭṭācārya. Calcutta, 1891, pp. 134.

Shakuntala, or the Recovered Ring. Translated by A. H. Edgren. New York, 1894, pp. 198.

Sakuntalā. Translation by Kālīpāda Mukerjee. In his Notes on Śakuntalā, Calcutta, 1895.

A literal English translation of Abhijñāna Śakuntalā with an introduction by T. R. Ratnam Aiyar. Madras, 1896, pp. 84.

Śakuntalā. Translated by Kalikes Banerji. Nadia (Bengal), 1901, pp. 166.

Śakuntalā. Translated by J. G. Jennings. Allahabad, 1902, pp. 217.

Śakuntalā: Idylls of Ancient Ind. By R. Vasudeva Row. Madras, 1903, pp. 6 + 94. [An attempt to render into idyllic poetry the subject of Kālidāsa's drama.]

Śakuntalā. Translated by A. M. Wright. Springfield, Mass., U. S. A., 1904, pp. 84.

B. French. Sacontala, ou l'anneau fatal, drame traduit de la langue sanscrit en Anglais, par Sir W. Jones, et de l'Anglais en Français par le citoyen A. Bruguière; avec des notes des traducteurs. Paris, 1803.

Gautier, Théophile. Sacountala, Ballet-Pantomime en deux actes tiré du drame de Calidasa. Musique de Reyer. Paris, 1859.

Fauche, Hippolyte. Oeuvres choisies de Kālidāsa. Śakuntalā. Paris, 1865.

La Reconnaissance de Sakountala, drame en sept actes de Kālidāsa, traduit du Sanskrit par P. E. Foucaux. 1° ed., Paris, 1867, pp. 24 + 188; 2° ed., 1874.

Sacountala. Traduite par Abel Bergaigne et P. Lehugeur. Paris, 1884, pp. 11 + 195.

L'anneau de Çakuntalā, comédie héroique. Traduite par A. Ferdinand Herold. Paris, 1896, pp. 161.

C. German. Sakontala, oder der Entscheidende Ring. Aus den Ursprachen Sanskrit und Prakrit ins Englische und aus diesem ins Deutsche übersetzt mit Erläuterungen von G. Forster. 1° ed., Mainz and Leipzig, 1791, pp. 40 + 366; 2° ed., Frankfurt-am-Main, 1803, pp. 44 + 267. Reprinted at Heidelberg, 1820, pp. 44 + 268, and at Leipzig, 1879, pp. 136.

Sakontala, oder der verhängnissvolle Ring; indisches Drama des Kalidas in sechs Aufzügen. Metrisch für die Bühne bearbeitet von Wilhelm Gerhard. Leipzig, 1820, pp. 16 + 190.

Sakuntala, oder der Erkennungsring, übersetzt von B. Hirzel. 1° ed., Zürich, 1833, pp. 29 + 155; 2° ed., 1849.

Śakuntalā von Höppl. 1854. [Free translation of the text.]

Śakuntala, ein indisches Schauspiel von Kalidasa, aus dem Sanskrit und Prakrit übersetzt und erläutert von Ernest Meier. In Die klassischen Dichtungen der Inder, 2. Theil, Stuttgart, 1847–54. Reprinted in Bibliothek ausländischer Klassiker, no. 58: 1° ed., Hildburgshausen, 1867; 2° ed., Leipzig, 1874.

Śakuntala, indisches Schauspiel von Kalidasa, metrisch übersetzt von Edmund Lobedanz. 1° ed., Leipzig, 1854, pp. 8 + 164; 2° ed., 1867; 3° ed., 1867, pp. 6 + 164; 4° ed., 1871; 6° ed., 1878; 7° ed., 1884.

Aus F. Rückert's Nachlass. Leipzig, 1867 and 1876. [Contains a translation of the Śakuntalā.]

Śakuntala, frei nach Kalidasa's altindischem Drama von A. Freiherrn von Wolzogen. Schwerin, 1869; Bühnenausgabe, Leipzig, 1879 (?), pp. 76.

Śakuntala. Metrisch frei bearbeitet von Arthur. Dresden, 1871.

Śakuntala. Für die deutschen Bühnen bearbeitet von A. Donsdorf. Wien, 1876, pp. 72.

Çakuntala, von Fr. Bodenstedt. Leipzig, 1887. [A romantic epic based on Kālidāsa's drama; cf. A. F. J. Remy, The Influence of India and Persia on the Poetry of Germany, New York, 1901, pp. 69–71.]

Śakuntala. Metrisch übersetzt von Ludwig Fritze. In his Indisches Theater, vol. 2, Chemnitz, 1877–79.

Śakuntala. Dichtung von Carl Wittkowsky. Musik von Ph. Scharwenka. Berlin, 1883, pp. 44.

Ballet in zwei Akten und fünf Bildern. Nach Kalidasa's Dichtung. Musik von S. Bachrich, in Scene gesetzt von Carl Telle. Vienna, 1884, pp. 16.

Śakuntalā. Deutsch von Hermann Camillo Kellner. Leipzig, 1890, pp. 111.

Śakuntalā. Indisches Schauspiel. Frei bearbeitet von G. Schmilinsky. Dresden, 1900, pp. 106.

Śakuntalā. Ein indisches Spiel. In deutscher Bühnenfassung von Max Möller. Berlin, 1902, pp. 7 + 117.

Śakuntalā. Romantisches Märchendrama in fünf Akten und einem Vorspiel, frei nach Kālidāsa für die deutschen Bühnen bearbeitet von Leopold von Schroeder. Munich, 1903, pp. 14 + 73.

D. Dutch. Sakontala, of de beslissende ring. Indisch schouspel. Mit opheld van G. Forster. Vertaald van E. M. Post. Haarlem, 1792.

Śakuntalā, of het Herkenningsteeken: Indisch tooneelspel in 7 bedrijven van Kālidāsa. Uit het Sanskrit vertaald door H. Kern. Haarlem, 1862.

E. Swedish. Śakuntalā; ett Indiskt dramatiskt Poem af Kalidas, öfversatt från Sanskrit på Engelska af W. Jones, och efter denne samt G. Forsters tyska tolkning på svenska af J. Ekelund. Stockholm, 1821, pp. 222.

Schakuṇtalā, eller den Förlorade Ringen. Ett indiskt skådespel af Kālidāsa från Sanskrit öfversatt och förklaradt af H. Edgren. Stockholm, 1875, pp. 184.

F. Danish. Sacontalā eller den uheldige Ring, et indiansk Drama af Cālidās; oversat af Original-Sprogene Sanscrit og Prāçrit i Engelsk; og heraf i Dansk med en Inleidning tel den danske Oversattelse. Copenhagen, 1793, pp. 71 + 230. [The translator was Hans West.]

Sakuntala, Skuespel i syv Optrin oversat og forklaret af Martin Hammerich. 1° ed., Copenhagen, 1845, pp. 16 + 139; 2° ed., 1858, pp. 170; 3° ed., 1879.

G. Icelandic. Śakuntalā. Translated by Dr. Steingrin Thoratainsohn.

H. Italian.[1] Śacontala, ossia L'Anello Fatale. Dramma tradotto dalla lingua orientale Sanskrit nell' idioma inglese dal Sig. W. Jones, indi dall' inglese in francese dal Sig. A. Bruguière, ultimamente dal francese in italiano da L. Doria. Con note. Darmstadt, 1815, pp. 15 + 214.

[1] There is also an unpublished Italian version of the Śakuntalā by Michele Kerbaker. See F. Cimmino, Il Tipo comico del "Vidūshaka" nell' antico dramma indiano, Naples, 1893, p. 2. n. 1.

Sacuntala riconosciuta per mezzo dell' anello. Dramma in sette atti. In Teatro scelto indiano, tradotto dal Sanscrito da Antonio Marazzi, vol. 1, Milan, 1871, pp. 9–176.

La Sacuntala di Calidasa, tradotta dal Sanscrito da O. Perini. Verona, 1873. In Versioni Indiane.

Sakuntala, dramma lirico da Alfredo Baccelli. Rome, 1888.

I. Spanish. Sakuntala, drama del poeta indio Kalidasa. Version directa del sanskrit por F. García Ayuso. Madrid, 1875. In Biblioteca Sanskrita.

J. Russian. Śakuntalā, indĕiskaya drama. Perevod s Sanskritskago Alex. Putyata. Moscow, 1879.

Sakuntala, Sanskritskaya drama v 7 dĕistviyakh. St. Petersburg. Desevaya Biblioteka, A. S. Suvorina, no. 252.

Śakuntalā. Drama v 7 dĕistviyakh. Perevod N. Volostskago. Vologda, 1890, pp. 179.

K. Polish. Sakontala czyli pierścień przeznaczenia: dramat indyjski w vii aktach z prologiem ze Sanskryckiego z rękopismu, wydal Hrabia J. Grabowski. (Objaśnienia przez J. Forstera.) Warsaw, 1861.

L. Hungarian. Śakuntalā. Translated by F. Karoly. Budapest, 1887.

M. Bohemian. Sakontalo: drama Indické od Kalidasy. Preložil C. Vyprpio. In Poesie Svetova, pt. 6, 1873, pp. 200.

N. Bengali. Śakuntalā, adapted from the Sanskrit drama of Kālidāsa by I. C. Vidyasagar. Calcutta, 1885.

Abhijñāna Śakuntalā. Translated into Bengali by J. N. Tagore. Calcutta, 1899, pp. 146.

O. Marathi. Shakuntala recognized by the ring. With a translation into Marathi by K. S. Rajvade. Bombay, 1869, pp. 11 + 267.

Śakuntalā with paraphrases in Sanskrit and in Marathi. Dharwar, 1882. In the Kāvyanāṭakādarśa.

Sangita Shakuntala Natak. Poona, 1887, pp. 176.

P. Hindi. Śakuntalā. Translated into Hindi. Critically edited with notes by Frederic Pincott. Text of K. L. Sinh. 1° ed., London, 1876, pp. 12 + 139. 2° ed., 1890.

Q. Hindustani. Śakuntalā translated into Hindustani from a Hindi version by Kazīm 'Alī Jawān. Lucknow, 1875, pp. 31.

R. Tamil. Śakuntalā. Traduction de la Version tamoule [by Rāmacandra or Rājanallūr] par Gérard Devèze. In Revue de Linguistique, 19 (1886), pp. 269–292, 361–380; 20 (1887), pp. 68–78, 114–129, 257–272, 352–376; 21 (1888), pp. 48–53.

S. Telugu. Śakuntalā. A new version in Telugu prose and verse by D. S. Pantulu. Madras, 1898, pp. 122.

Criticism. Notes on Śakuntalā. In Bengali, English, and Sanskrit. Calcutta, 1895, pp. 323.

Berchet, Giovanni. Saggio sul dramma indiano la Sacontala, ossia l'Anello Fatale, di Calidasa. Milan (?), 1818. [In the Conciliatore under pseudonym of Grisostomo.]

Böhtlingk, Otto von. Einige Nachträge zu meiner Ausgabe der Ring-Çakuntalā. In Bulletin de la classe des sciences historiques, philosophiques et politiques de l'Académie de St. Petersbourg, 2, p. 119.

Bollensen, Fr. Die Recensionen der Sakuntala. In Nachrichten der Gesellschaft der Wissenschaften zu Göttingen, June 23, 1880.

Borooah, Anundoram. A Companion to the Sanskrit-reading Undergraduates of Calcutta University. Part 4, on the Abhijñāna Śakuntalā of Kālidāsa. Calcutta, 1878, pp. 6 + 58.

Burkhard, C. Die Kaçmīrer Çakuntalā-Handschrift. Vienna, 1884, pp. 163.

Burkhard, C. Lectiones codicis Çākuntali Bikānīrensis. Vienna, 1882, pp. 16. Progr. d. Franz-Josephs Gymn.

Burkhard, C. Flexiones Prācriticae quas editioni suae Sācuntali pro supplemento adjecit. Breslau, 1874, pp. 9 + 41.

Chézy, A. L. Notes et corrections supplémentaires pour l'édition in 4° du drame indien de Cālidāsa intitulé La Reconaissance de Sacountala donnée en 1830. Paris, 1831, pp. 49.

Cappeller, C. [Review of the editions of the Śakuntalā by Pischel and Williams, and of the translations by Rückert and Fritze] in Jenaer Literaturzeitung, 1877, Art. 117.

Gilchrist, J. B. Sukoontala Natuk; being an Appendix to the English and Hindoostanee Dialogues in the Universal Character. London, 1826, pp. 20 + 104.

Gubernatis, A. de. Sacountalā et Griselda. In Verh. des 13. intern. Orientalisten-Kongr. (1902), Leiden, 1904, pp. 21–24.

Hamaker, H. A. Over de Sakontala van Calidas. In Mnemosyne, 2 (1823), p. 213.

Hedrström, O. F. Om Sakuntala. Upsala, 1875.

Kālīpāda Mukerjee. Notes on Śakuntalā. 1. Notes; 2. Translation; 3. Appendices. Calcutta, 1895, pp. 325.

Müller, B. Kālidāsa's Çakuntalā und ihre Quelle. Breslau, 1874, pp. 20. [Programm.]

Pischel, R. De Kālidāsae Çākuntali recensionibus (Particula prima). Breslau, 1870, pp. 67.

Pischel, R. Die Recensionen der Çakuntalā. Eine Antwort an Herrn Prof. A. Weber. Breslau, 1875, pp. 27.

Rabe, C. De Calidasae Sacuntala. Breslau, 1845, pp. 35.

Ryder, Arthur W. Kṛṣṇanātha's Commentary on the Bengal Recension of the Çakuntalā. In JAOS. 23 (1902), pp. 79–83.

Sarkār, Vihārī Lāl. Sakuntalā-Rahasya. The true import of the Sakuntalā. Calcutta, 1896, pp. 144. [In Bengali.]

Schuyler, Montgomery, Jr. The Editions and Translations of Śakuntalā. In JAOS. 22 (1901), pp. 237–248.

Weber, A. Die Recensionen der Çakuntalā. In Indische Studien, 14 (1876), pp. 35–69, 161–311.

Wilson, H. H. Sur un drame indien; extrait du Calcutta Annual Register, et traduit par M. Dondey-Dupré fils. In JA. 1° series, vol. 10 (1827), pp. 174–179.

Vikramorvaśī troṭaka. *Manuscripts.* A 1. p. 569 = 50 Mss. and 2 Com.; by Abbayācaraṇa 1, by Kāṭayavema 2, by Raṅganātha 3, by Rāmamaya 1; A 2. p. 134 = 7 Mss. and Com. by Kāṭayavema 1, by Raṅganātha 3; A 3. p. 120 = 2 Mss. and Com. by Kāṭayavema 1; Hz. 3. 1774; IO. 7. 4120; TT. 66; Com. by Kāṭayavema, Hz. 3. 1755; Com. by Raṅganātha, IO. 7. 4121.

Text Editions. Vikramorvaśī. With a commentary explanatory of the Prākrit passages. Calcutta, 1830, pp. 122.

Urvasia, Fabula Calidasi. Textum sancritum edidit, interpretationem latinam et notas illustrantes adjecit Robertus Lenz. Berlin, 1833, pp. 25 + 238.

Vikramorvaśī, das ist, Urwasi, der Preis der Tapferkeit, ein Drama Kalidasa's, in fünf Akten. Herausgegeben, übersetzt und erläutert von F. Bollensen. St. Petersburg, 1846, pp 17 + 608 + 88.

Vikramorvaśī. Edited by M. Monier Williams. Hertford, 1849. [Prākrit passages in Sanskrit only.]

Vikramorvaśī. Edited with a commentary of the Prākrit passages. Bombay, 1859, pp. 119.

Vikramorvaśī. Edited by R. Tarkaratna. Calcutta, 1868.

Vikramorvaśī. Edited with notes by R. Śarman. Calcutta, 1869, pp. 2 + 155.

Vikramorvaśī. Calcutta, 1870, pp. 67. [Prākrit passages in Sanskrit only.]

Vikramorvaśī. Edited with the commentary of Tārānātha Śarman by J. Vidyāsāgara. Calcutta, 1873, pp. 184.

Vikramorvaśīyam, herausgegeben nach drāviḍischen Handschriften von R. Pischel. In Monatsb. der Königl. Akad. der Wiss. zu Berlin, 1875 (1876), pp. 609–670.

Vikramorvaśīyam. Edited with English notes by S. P. Pandit. 1° ed., Bombay, 1879, pp. 12 + 162; 2° ed., 1889, pp. 310; 3° ed., 1901. Bombay Sanskrit Series, no. 16.

Vikramorvaśī. Little Conjevaram, 1883, pp. 60.

Vikramorvaśī, with interpretation of the Prākrit passages. Vizagapatam, 1883, pp. 118.

Vikramorvaśī, with a commentary. Edited by P. C. N. Charya. Vizagapatam, 1883, pp. 180.

Vikramorvaśī, with commentary. Madras, 1884, pp. 24.

Vikramorvaśīya, with the commentary of Raṅganātha. Edited by K. P. Parab and M. R. Telang. 1° ed., Bombay, 1888, pp. 148; 2° ed., 1889, pp. 310.

Vikramorvaśīyam. The Student's Practical Edition with Sanskrit

Text, English Translation, and Notes by G. B. Vaidya. Bombay, 1894, pp. 12 + 96 + 216.

Vikramorvaśī. Edited with an elucidary commentary in Sanskrit by M. R. Kāle. Bombay, 1895, pp. 173.

Vikramorvaśīya with the commentary Arthaprakāśikā. Edited with an English translation, critical and explanatory notes, and various readings by M. R. Kāle. 1° ed., Bombay, 1898, pp. 374; 2° ed., 1903, pp. 374.

Vikramorvaśīyam. With Sanskrit text, English translations, copious notes, and an elaborate introduction, by K. B. Parānjpe. Bombay, 1898, pp. 264.

Translations. A. English. Vikrama and Urvaśī, or the Hero and the Nymph. Translated by Wilson, 1, pp. 183–274.

Vikramorvaśī. Translated into English prose by E. B. Cowell. Hertford, 1851.

Vikramorvaśī. Translated into English lyrical verse by Brajendranath De. Canto 1. In Calcutta Review, Oct. 1884, pp. 440–442.

Urvasie. In English poetry by Aurobind Ghose. Bombay, 1899, pp. 39.

B. French. Vikramorvaçi. Ourvaçi donnée pour prix de l'héroisme. Drame traduit du Sanscrit par P. E. Foucaux. 1° ed., Paris, 1861, pp. 96; 2° ed., 1879, pp. 137. Bibl. Orient. Elzévir., no. 26.

C. German. Urwasi, der Preis der Tapferkeit. Ein indisches Schauspiel. Aus dem Sanskrit und Prākrit übersetzt von K. G. A. Hoefer. Berlin, 1837, pp. 8 + 100.

Urwasi und der Held. Indisches Melodram von Kalidasa, dem Dichter der Sakuntala. Aus dem Sanskrit und Prākrit metrisch übersetzt von B. Hirzel. Frauenfeld, 1838, pp. 30 + 164.

Urvasi. Deutsch metrisch bearbeitet von E. Lobedanz. 1° ed., Leipzig, 1861, pp. 14 + 115; 3° ed., 1884.

Urvasi, ein indisches Schauspiel von Kalidasa, metrisch übersetzt von Ludwig Fritze. Leipzig, 1880, pp. 80.

D. Swedish. Vikramorvaçi. Öfversatt och förklaradt af C. J. Bergstedt. Stockholm, 1846.

Vikramorvaci. Öfversatt af A. J. Callin. Helsingborg, 1866.

E. Italian. Vikramorvasi, dramma tradotto di Francesco Cimmino. Turin, 1890, pp. 79.

F. Spanish. Vikramorvasi, drama del poeta indio Kalidasa. Version directa del Sanskrit por F. García Ayuso. Madrid, 1874, pp. 136. In Biblioteca Sanskrita.

G. Bohemian. Urvasi. Drama v pěti jednánich od Kalidasy. Emanuel Fait. Prague, 1890, pp. 10. [Program of the Czech Realgymnasium.]

H. Bengali. Vikramorvaśī, translated into Bengali by K. Singh. Calcutta, 1857.

I. Gujarati. Vikramorvaśī. Translated into Gujarati by R. Udayarāma. Bombay, 1868.

Vikramorvashīya. A Sanskrit drama in 5 acts translated into Gujarati prose and verse with critical, explanatory, and mythological notes, and a complete life of the poet, by K. G. Bhatt. Bombay, 1898, pp. 258.

Criticism. Lenz, Robert. Apparatus criticus ad Urvasiam fabulam Calidasi, quem tamquam suae eius libri editionis appendicem Londinii conscripsit. Berlin, 1834, pp. 36.

Collected Works of Kālidāsa. Oeuvres complètes de Kālidāsa traduites du sanscrit en français pour la première fois par Hippolyte Fauche. Paris, 1859–60, 2 vols.

Teatro scelto indiano, tradotto dal Sanscrito da Antonio Marazzi. Vol. 1. Teatro di Calidasa. Milan, 1871, pp. 429.

Mahākavi Kālidāser Granthāvalī. Edited by N. K. Basu. Calcutta, 1892.

Mahākavi Kālidāser Granthāvalī. The works of the great poet Kālidāsa. Edited by U. N. Mukherji. 2° ed., Calcutta, 1896, pp. 1356.

Works of Kālidāsa. Translated into English. Calcutta, 1901, 2 vols.

General Criticism of Kālidāsa. Bendall, Cecil. Kālidāsa in Ceylon. In JRAS. N.S. 20 (1888), p. 440.

Bhāu Dājī. On the Sanscrit Poet Kālidāsa. In JRASBo. 6 (1861), pp. 19–30, 207–230.

Grierson, G. A. Are Kālidāsa's Heroes monogamists? In JASBe. 46 (1877), pp. 39–40.

Grierson, G. A. Some Further Notes on Kālidāsa. Calcutta, 1879, pp. 46.

Grierson, G. A. Some Further Notes on Kālidāsa. In JASBe. 48 (1879), pp. 32–48.

Harris, Ch. An Investigation of some of Kālidāsa's Views. Evansville, Ohio, 1884, pp. 58.

Huth, G. Die Zeit des Kālidāsa. Mit einem Anhang: Zur Chronologie der Werke des Kālidāsa. Berlin, 1890, pp. 68.

Jackson, A. V. Williams. Kālidāsa. In Warner's Library of the World's Best Literature, vol. 15. New York, 1897.

Jackson, A. V. Williams. Time Analysis of Sanskrit Plays, 1. The Dramas of Kālidāsa. In JAOS. 20 (1899), pp. 341–359.

Jackson, A. V. Williams. Notes from India, 1. A legend of Kālidāsa preserved at Ujjain. In JAOS. 22 (1901), pp. 331–332.

Jacobi, H. The Date of Kālidāsa. In IA. 19 (1890), p. 285.

Leonard, G. S. Further Proofs of the Polygamy of Kālidāsa's Heroes. In JASBe. 46 (1877), pp. 160–163.

Liebich, B. Das Datum Candragomin's und Kalidasa's. In Jahresbericht der Schlesischen Gesellschaft für vaterländische Kultur, Orient-sprachwiss. Sektion. Breslau, 1903, pp. 11.

Nève, F. Calidasa dans les raffinements de sa culture. Paris, 1864.

Pischel, R. Neue Bruchstücke des Sanskritkanons der Buddhisten aus Idykutšari, Chinesisch-Turkestān, mit drei Tafeln. In Sitzungsb. der kgl. Preuss. Akad. der Wiss. 39 (1904), pp. 1138–1145. [A fragment quoted p. 1144 connects Kālidāsa with the court of King Bhoja. Cf. Kielhorn in The Academy, June 16, 1894, vol. 45, pp. 498–499.]

Pathak, K. B. On the date of Kālidāsa. In JRASBo. 19 (1895), pp. 35–43.

Prannāth Paṇḍit. Morals of Kālidāsa. In JASBe. 45 (1876), pp. 352–367.

Summer, Mary. Les héroines de Kalidasa et celles de Shakespeare. Paris, 1879. Bibl. Orient. Elzévir., no. 24.
J. E. Seneviratne. The life of Kalidas. Colombo, 1901, pp. 5 + 35.
R. V. Tullu. Traditionary Account of Kālidāsa. In IA. 7 (1878), pp. 115–117.

Kālidāsa Prahasananāṭaka. Madras, 1883, pp. 30.
Kālidāsaprahasana A 1. p. 99. *See also* Kāśīdāsaprahasana.
Kalikeḷiprahasana (vaikṛta) mentioned in RS.
Kalyāṇīpariṇaya A 1. p. 86 = 2 Mss.
Kāmadattā bhāṇikā mentioned in SD. 556.
Kāmadatta dhūrtaprakaraṇa mentioned in RS.
Kāmākṣīpariṇaya A 1. p. 94.
Kamalākaṇṭhīrava *see* **Nārāyaṇa.**
Kamalāvilāsa *see* **Śivanārāyaṇadāsa.**
Kamalinīkalahaṃsa *see* **Cūḍāmaṇi Dīkṣita.**
Kāmavilāsa *see* **Veṅkappa.**
Kampanīpratāpamaṇḍana *see* **Bindumādhava.**
Kaṃsavadha *see* **Dāmodara** *and* **Śeṣakṛṣṇa.**
Kanakavallīpariṇaya A 1. p. 78.
Kanakāvatīmādhava śilpaka mentioned in SD. 551.
Kāñcanācārya Dhanaṃjayavijaya vyāyoga A 1. p. 266 = 14 Mss.; A 2. p. 57; A 3. p. 58 = 1 Ms. and Com. by Rāmakṛṣṇa 1; CS. 226. Analyzed by Wilson, 2, p. 374.
Idem Dhanaṃjayavijaya, a comedy in one act by Kāñcana Ācārya. Bombay, 1856, pp. 10.
Idem Dhanaṃjayavijaya. Edited by T. Tarkavacaspati. 1° ed., Calcutta, 1857, pp. 26; 2° ed., 1871, pp. 36.
Idem Dhanaṃjayavijaya. Mysore, 1880, pp. 26.
Idem Dhanaṃjayavijaya. Edited by Śivadatta and Parab. Bombay, 1895, pp. 3 + 20. Kāvyamālā, no. 54.
Kandarpadarpaṇa *see* **Śrīkaṇṭha** *and* **Veṅkaṭa Kavi.**
Kandarpakeli prahasana mentioned in SD. 534–535.
Kāntimatīpariṇaya *see* **Cokkanātha.**

Kanyāmādhava A 1. p. 79.
Karṇasundarī *see* **Bilhaṇa.**
Karpūramañjarī *see* **Rājaśekhara.**
Karuṇakandaḷa mentioned in RS.
Kāśīdāsaprahasana A 1. p. 104. *See also* Kālidāsaprahasana.
Kāśīpati Mukundānanda bhāṇa A 1. p. 459 = 15 Mss.; A 2. pp. 106, 217 = 3 Mss.; A 3. p. 99; IO. 7. 4195.
Idem Mukundānanda. Edited by Moḍaka and Sāne. Poona, 1878. In Kāvyetihāsasaṃgraha, 1, pts. 1–5.
Idem Mukundānanda. A monologue drama on the adventures of a loose character. Madras, 1882, pp. 78.
Idem Mukundānanda. Edited by Durgāprasāda and Parab. Bombay, 1889, pp. 3 + 74. Kāvyamālā, no. 16.
Kāśyapa Abhinavakālidāsa Śṛṅgārakośa bhāṇa A 1. p. 660.
Kaumudīsudhākara *see* **Tarkālaṃkāra.**
Kauśika Nallābudha Śṛṅgārasarvasva bhāṇa A 1. p. 661.
Idem Śṛṅgārasarvasva. Edited by Durgāprasāda and Parab. Bombay, 1902, pp. 5 + 38. Kāvyamālā, no. 78.
Kautukaratnākara prahasana A 1. p. 131; A 2. p. 25 = IO. 7. 4197. Analyzed by Cappeller in Gurupūjākaumudī, Festgabe für Weber, Leipzig, 1896, pp. 62–63.
Kautukasarvasva *see* **Gopīnātha.**
Kavibhūṣaṇa Adbhutārṇava A 3. p. 2.
Kavikarṇapūra (born in 1525) Caitanyacandrodaya A 1. p. 190 = 3 Mss.; A 2. p. 200; A 3. p. 41; CS. 225; SCBen. 796.
Idem Chaitanya Chandroday Natak. In Sanskrit and Bengali. Calcutta, 1853, pp. 490.
Idem Caitanyacandrodaya, or the incarnation of Caitanya, a drama in ten acts. With a comment explanatory of the Prākrita passages by Viśvanātha Śāstri. Edited by R. Mitra. Calcutta, 1854. In Bibl. Indica.
Idem Caitanyacandrodaya. Edited with a commentary by J. Vidyāsāgara. Calcutta, 1885, pp. 452.
Kavi Paṇḍita Hṛdayavinoda prahasana A 2. p. 237.
Kaviputra, a dramatist, mentioned in the prologue of the Māla-

vikāgnimitra of Kālidāsa.
Kaviśekhara *see* **Jyotirīśvara.**
Kavīśvara Mādhavānala A 1. p. 450.
Kavitārkikasiṃha Rukmiṇīpariṇaya A 2. p. 123.
Keliraivataka hallīśa mentioned in SD. 555.
Keralābharaṇa *see* **Rāmacandra Dīkṣita.**
Keśavacarita mentioned in the Nāṭakacandrikā.
Keśavanātha Godāpariṇaya A 1. p. 159 = 5 Mss.
Kiṃpaca A 1. p. 106.
Krīḍārasātala śrīgadita mentioned in SD. 550.
Kṛṣṇa *or* **Kṛṣṇakavi** *see* **Śeṣakṛṣṇa.**
Kṛṣṇabhakticandrikā *see* **Anantadeva.**
Kṛṣṇābhyudaya *see* **Lokanatha.**
Kṛṣṇadatta Maithila (first part of 17th century) Kuvalayāśvīya A 1. p. 113.
Idem Purañjanacarita A 1. p. 339.
Idem Sāndrakutūhala prahasana A 1. p. 707.
Kṛṣṇakavīndra (perhaps the same as **Śeṣakṛṣṇa,** cf. A 1. p. 117) Satyabhāmāvilāsa *or* Satyabhāmāpariṇaya A 1. p. 689.
Kṛṣṇakaviśekhara (wrote before 1643) Kuvalayavatī nāṭikā A 3. p. 25 = IO. 7. 4184.
Kṛṣṇakutūhala *see* **Madhusūdana Sarasvatī.**
Kṛṣṇalīlā *see* **Vaidyanātha.**
Kṛṣṇalīlātaraṅgiṇī *see* **Nārāyaṇatīrtha.**
Kṛṣṇamacari R. Vāsantikāsvapna. An adaptation of Shakespeare's Midsummer Night's Dream. A Sanskrit drama in five acts. Kumbhakonam, 1892, pp. 15 + 71.

Kṛṣṇamiśra (2d half of 11th century), son of Viṣṇu, wrote for King Kīrtivarmadeva.

Prabodhacandrodaya. *Manuscripts.* A 1. p. 352 = 75 Mss. and 9 Com.; by Appayya Dīkṣita 3, by Gaṇeśa 1, by Mathurānātha 1, by Maheśvara 1, by Rāmadāsa 14, by Rudradeva 2, by Sadātman 1; A 2. pp. 78, 211 = 15 Mss. and 2 Com.; by Gaṇeśa 2, by Rāmadāsa 4, by Subrahmaṇya 2, by Govinda 1; A 3. p. 75 = 20 Mss. and Com.

by Gaṇeśa 2, by Devarāja 1, by Rāmadāsa 8; SCBen. 693; Weber 1357 (in Bhāṣā); Hz. 3. 1578; IO. 7. 4138, 4139, 4140, 4141, 4143; TT. 68; Com. by Ghanaśyāma, Hz. 3. 1583; Com. by Ganeśa, IO. 7. 4143; Com. by Govinda, IO. 7. 4144; Com. by Rāmadāsa, IO. 7. 4139, 4140, 4141, 4142, 4143; Com., SCBen. 693.

Text Editions. Prabodhacandrodaya, with a commentary by Maheśvara Nyāyālaṃkāra. Edited by Bhavānīcaraṇa Śarman. Calcutta, 1832, pp. 54. [In Bengali characters.]

Prabodhacandrodaya. Sanscrite cum scholiis et variis lectionibus edidit H. Brockhaus. Leipzig, 1835–1845, pp. 8 + 254. [Contains the commentaries of Rāmadāsa and Maheśvara Nyāyālaṃkāra.]

Prabodhacandrodaya, with the commentary of Nyāyālaṃkāra. Calcutta, 1838.

Prabodhacandrodaya. Poona, 1851.

Prabodhacandrodaya, with the commentary of Nyāyālaṃkara. Edited by J. Vidyāsāgara. Calcutta, 1874, pp. 135.

Prabodhacandrodaya. With Rāmadāsa's commentary called Prakāśa. Edited by S. Tiruveṅkaṭācārya. Madras, 1876, pp. 3 + 166.

Prabodhacandrodaya, with Rāmadāsa's Prakāśa, revised by Tryambaka Gondhaḷekhara. 2° ed., Poona, 1881, pp. 136.

Prabodhacandrodaya, with the commentary Prakāśa. Madras, 1884, pp. 166.

Prabodhacandrodaya, edited with a commentary by R. V. Dīkṣit. Poona, 1886, pp. 178.

Prabodhacandrodaya. Edited by Adyānāth Vidyābhūṣan. Shibpur, 1894, pp. 168.

Prabodhacandrodaya. With a commentary by Maheśvara Nyāyālaṃkāra, edited by Pandit H. Śāstri. Calcutta, 1895, pp. 161.

Prabodhacandrodaya with the commentary Candrikā. Bombay, 1898, pp. 251.

Translations. A. English. Prabodha Candrodaya, or Rise of the Moon of Intellect, a spiritual drama, and Ātma Bodha, or the Knowledge of the Spirit. Translated from the Sanskrit by J. Taylor, M.D. 1° ed., Bombay, 1812; 2° ed., Calcutta, 1854, pp. 13 + 125; 3° ed., Bombay, 1893, pp. 18 + 74.

Prabodhacandrodaya. Translated by Gaṅgādhar Nyāyaratna. Calcutta, 1852. [English translation?]

B. French. Le Lever de la lune de la connaissance. Traduction de la Prabodhacandrodaya sanscrite par S. Devèze. In Revue de Ling. 32 (1899), pp. 230–246; 33 (1900), pp. 67–86, 223–239; 34 (1901), pp. 240–254; 35 (1902), pp. 27–40, 195–211; 36 (1903), pp. 139–159, 226–245.

C. German. Prabod'h Chandro'daya, das ist, der Aufgang des Mondes der Erkenntniss, ein allegorisches Drama. Nach der englischen Übersetzung des Dr. J. Taylor von J. G. Rhode. In Beiträge zur Alterthumskunde mit besonderer Rücksicht auf das Morgenland, Berlin, 1820, 2, pp. 41–99. [First three acts.]

Prabodhacandrodaya. Die Geburt des Begriffs. Ein theologisch-philosophiches Drama, zum ersten Male ins Deutsch übersetzt; mit einem Vorwort eingeführt von K. Rosenkranz. Königsberg, 1842, pp. 25 + 183. [Translated by Th. Goldstücker; published without his name.]

Prabodhacandrodaya, oder der Erkenntnissmondaufgang. Philosophisches Drama. Nebst Kalidasa, Meghadūta. Metrisch übersetzt von B. Hirzel. Zürich, 1846.

D. Dutch. De Maan der Kennis. Theologisch-metaphysisch Drama. Vertaald door P. A. S. van Limburg Brouwer. Amsterdam, 1869.

E. Russian. Toryestvo svĕtloi mysli. Drama v šest' aktakh. Perevod s Sanskritskago. Moscow, 1847, pp. 20 + 194. Moskovski naučny i literaturny sbornik, vol. 18.

F. Bengali. Atmatattvakaumudi, being a paraphrase of the Prabodhacandrodaya in Bengali, by K. Tarkapañcānana, G. Gaṅgādhar and R. Śiromaṇi. Calcutta, 1822, pp. 194, with the verses of the original in Sanskrit; 2° ed., 1855, pp. 190; 3° ed., 1861, pp. 168.

Prabodh Chandroday. Translated from Sanskrit by Gaṅgādhar Nyāyāratna. Calcutta, 1852. [Bengali translation?]

G. Hindustani. Tahṣ̄īl-i makāl, also called Ta'wīd-i Īmān. Translated by Ākā Ḥasan. Gujranwala, 1871, pp. 60.

Criticism. Schuyler, Montgomery, Jr. A Bibliography of the Plays of Bhavabhūti and of Kṛṣṇamiśra. In JAOS. 25 (1904), pp. 189–196.

Kṛṣṇamiśra Vīravijaya īhāmṛga A 1. p. 595.

Kṛṣṇānanda Vācaspati Antar Vyākaraṇa Nāṭyapariśiṣṭa. A drama embodying grammar. Calcutta, 1894–1896, 2 pts., pp. 131 + 303.

Kṛṣṇānanda Bhaṭṭācārya Nāṭyapariśiṣṭa, *i. e.*, an appendix to dramatic literature. Lessons in Sanskrit grammar disguised in the form of a dramatic entertainment. With two commentaries. Calcutta, 1840, pp. 152.

Idem Nāṭyapariśiṣṭa. A grammatical commentary containing discussions on the subject of Sanskrit inflexion. Calcutta, 1855, pp. 125.

Kṛṣṇanātha Sarvabhaumabhaṭṭācārya Ānandalatikā IO. 7. 4203.

Kṛṣṇarāya (16th century) Jāmbavatīkalyāṇa A 1. p. 206.

Kṛṣṇa Sūri Draupadīpariṇaya A 2. p. 57.

Kṛtārthamādhava *see* **Rāmamāṇika.**

Kṛtyarāvaṇa quoted in SD. 423.

Kṣemacandrabodha A 1. p. 134.

Kṣemendra Vyāsadāsa (11th century) Citrabhārata mentioned in his Aucityavicāracarcā 31 and Kavikaṇṭhābharaṇa 5. 1.

Idem Lalitaratnamālā mentioned in his Aucityavicāracarcā 21.

Kṣemīśvara.

Caṇḍakauśika. *Manuscripts.* A 1. p. 175 = 16 Mss.; A 2. p. 35 = 4 Mss.; A 3. p. 38; CS. 222, 223; Hz. 3. 2020.

Text Editions. Caṇḍakauśika, *i. e.*, the Fierceness of Kauśika. A drama in five acts. Bombay, 1860, pp. 23.

Caṇḍakauśika. Edited with a commentary and translation of the Prākrit passages by J. Tarkālaṃkāra. Calcutta, 1867, pp. 5 + 113.

Chanda Kousika. A Drama by Arya Kshemishwara, edited with a commentary by J. Vidyāsāgara. Calcutta, 1884, pp. 138.

Translation. Kausika's Zorn. Ein indisches Drama von Kschemisvara. Zum ersten Mal und metrisch übersetzt von Ludwig Fritze. Leipzig, 1882, pp. 85.

Criticism. Cimmino, Francesco. Studii sul teatro indiano. 2. Sul dramma Caṇḍakauśika. In Rendiconto dell' Accademia di Archeologia, Lettere e Belle Arti (di Napoli), 19 (1905), pp. 31–76.

Naiṣadhānanda A 1. p. 306 = 2 Mss., but cf. A 1. p. 134.

Kulapatyaṅka quoted in SD. 473. This may be only an act of a play.

Kumāranarendrasāha Muditamadālasa A 1. p. 461.

Kumāratātaya Pārijāta A 1. p. 335.

Kumāravijaya *see* **Ghanaśyāma.**

Kumbha quoted in SD. 476.

Kumudacandra *see* **Yaśaścandra.**

Kundamālā quoted in SD. 291.

Kuṇḍamālā *see* **Nāgayya.**

Kuśakumudvatīya *see* **Atirātrayājin.**

Kuśalavavijaya *see* **Veṅkaṭa Kṛṣṇa Dīkṣita.**

Kusumabāṇavilāsa bhāṇa A 1. p. 113.

Kusumaśekharavijaya īhāmṛga mentioned in SD. 518.

Kuvalayāśvacarita *see* **Lakṣmaṇamāṇikya.**

Kuvalayāśvamadālasa *see* **Vaṃśamaṇi.**

Kuvalayāśvīya *see* **Kṛṣṇadatta.**

Kuvalayavatī *see* **Kṛṣṇakaviśekhara.**

L

Laghuvyāsa Vṛttivallabha A 1. p. 541.

Lakṣmaṇamāṇikya Kuvalayāśvacarita A 3. p. 25.

Lakṣmaṇamāṇikyadeva Vikhyātavijaya A 3. p. 120.

Lakṣmīnṛsiṃha Kavi Anaṅgasarvasva bhāṇa A 1. p. 12.
Lakṣmīsvayaṃvara *see* **Śrīnivāsa Catuṣkavīndradāsa.**
Lalitamādhava SCBen. 799 (with Com.)
Lalitamādhava *see* **Rūpa Gosvāmin.**
Lalitaratnamālā *see* **Kṣemendra.**
Lalitavigraharāja *see* **Somadeva.**
Lambodara prahasana A 1. p. 542.
Laṭakamelaka *see* **Śaṅkhadhara.**
Lavalīpariṇaya *see* **Appāśāstrin.**
Līlāmadhukara bhāṇa mentioned in SD. 513.
Liṅgadurbheda *see* **Dāḍima.**
Liṅgaguṇṭamarāma Śṛṅgārarasodaya miśrabhāṇa A 1. p. 661.
Lokānanda *see* **Candragomin.**
Lokanātha Bhaṭṭa Kṛṣṇābhyudaya prekṣaṇaka A 1. p. 124.

M

Madālasa *see* **Rāma Bhaṭṭa.**
Madālasā *see* **Gokulanātha.**
Madālasāpariṇaya A 1. p. 426.
Madanabhūṣaṇa bhāṇa A 1. p. 425.
Madanagopālavilāsa *see* **Rāma Kavi.**
Madanamañjarī *see* **Viḷinātha.**
Madanasaṃjīvana *see* **Ghanaśyāma.**
Mādhava Bhaṭṭa Subhadrāharaṇa. A Śrīgadita, or short drama in one act, on the story of Subhadrā, wife of Arjuna. Edited by Durgāprasāda and Parab. Bombay, 1888, pp. 3 + 20. Kāvyamālā, no. 9.
Mādhavānala A 1. p. 450 = 2 Mss.
Mādhavānala *see* **Ānandadhara** *and* **Kavīśvara.**
Mādhavī vīthikā mentioned in RS.
Madhumālatī A 1. p. 426.
Madhumathanavijaya quoted in Kāvyāloka, p. 152 (A 2. p. 97).
Madhurāniruddha *see* **Candraśekhara Rāyaguru.**
Madhusūdana redactor of the more recent version of the Mahānāṭaka of **Hanuman.**

Madhusūdana Sarasvatī Kṛṣṇakutūhala A 1. p. 119 = 3 Mss
Idem Viṣṇukutūhala mentioned in DR. intr. p. 30. [Perhaps a mistake for the preceding.]
Mahādeva, son of Kṛṣṇasūri, Adbhutadarpaṇa A 1. p. 8 = 3 Mss.
Idem Adbhutadarpaṇa. Edited by Durgāprasāda and Parab. Bombay, 1896, pp. 3 + 124 + 4. Kāvyamālā, no. 55.
Mahādeva Kavīśācārya Sarasvatī Dānakelikaumudī bhāṇikā A 1. p. 249.
Mahādeva Śāstrin Unmattarāghava A 1. p. 66.
Mahādeva *see also* **Maheśvara.**
Mahānāṭaka *see* **Hanuman.**
Mahāvīracarita *see* **Bhavabhūti.**
Mahāvīrānanda *or* Vīrānanda mentioned in RS. and in DR. intr. p. 30.
Maheśa Paṇḍita Svarṇamuktāvivāda IO. 7. 4202.
Idem Svarṇamuktāvivāda. Bombay. In Kāvyetihāsasaṃgraha, vol. 10.
Maheśvara *or* **Mahādeva** Dhūrtaviḍambana prahasana A 1. p. 272.
Māheśvara Sabhā A 1. p. 696.
Maheśvarānanda mentioned in RS.
Maheśvarātmaja Śaṅkaralāla Sāvitrīcarita chāyānāṭaka. An original play in seven acts, on the myth of Sāvitrī, daughter of Aśvapati. Bombay, 1882, pp. 14 + 324.
Mahiṣamaṅgala bhāṇa. A short drama on an incident occurring in a village called Mahiṣamaṅgala, apparently written by an inhabitant of the place. With a commentary. Palghat, 1890, pp. 84.
Maikela Madhresūdanadatta Śarmiṇiṣṭha. 2° ed., Calcutta, 1854 (1270 A. H.), pp. 84.
Maithilīpariṇaya *see* **Hastimallasena.**
Maithilīya *see* **Nārāyaṇa Śāstrin.**
Makhin *see* **Anandarāya Makhin.**
Mālamaṅgalabhāṇa (by Mālamaṅgala ?) A 1. p. 453.

Mālamaṅgalabhāṇa. A short dramatic monologue in verse. Olavakod, 1887, pp. 40.

Mālatīmādhava *see* **Bhavabhūti.**

Mālavikāgnimitra *see* **Kālidāsa.**

Mallasena *see* **Hastimallasena.**

Mallāsomayājin *or* **Somayājin** Jīvanmuktikalyāṇa A 1. p. 207.

Mallikāmāruta *see* **Uddaṇḍin.**

Maṅgala *see* **Jīvānanda Jyotirvid.**

Maṇika (end of 14th century) Abhinavarāghavānanda L. app. p. 73.

Mañjulanaiṣadha *see* **Paravastu.**

Manmathonmathana *see* **Rāma.**

Mantrāṅga A 1. p. 431 = 2 Mss.

Mantrin Yaśaḥpāla *see* **Yaśaḥpāla.**

Maratakavallīpariṇaya *see* **Śrīnivāsadāsa.**

Mathurādāsa Vṛṣabhānujā nāṭikā A 1. p. 599 = 4 Mss.; A 2. p. 143.

Idem Vṛṣabhānujā. A drama in four acts. Edited by B. Tripāṭhi. Benares, 1867–1869. In The Pandit, old series, vols. 2, 4.

Idem Vṛṣabhānujā. Edited by Śivadatta and Parab. Bombay, 1895, pp. 3 + 60. Kāvyamālā, no. 46.

Mathurānāṭaka *see* **Candraśekhara Rāyaguru.**

Mātrarāja Anaṅgaharṣa (9th century?) Tāpasavatsarāja A 1. p. 228; A 2. p. 48.

Māyākāpālika saṃlāpaka mentioned in SD. 549.

Māyākuraṅgikā īhāmṛga mentioned in RS.

Māyurāja Udāttarāghava mentioned by Dhanika on DR. 2.54; 3. 3, 22.

Megheśvara *see* **Hastimallasena.**

Menakāhita rāsaka mentioned in SD. 548.

Meṇṭha *see* **Bhartṛmeṇṭha.**

Miśrabhāṇa *see* **Gundarāma.**

Mithyācāra *see* **Vaidyanātha.**

Mithyājñānakhaṇḍana *or* Mithyājñānaviḍambana *see* **Ravidāsa.**

Moharājaparājaya *see* **Yaśaḥpāla.**

Mokṣāditya Bhīmavikrama vyāyoga (composed in 1328) CBMMS. 273.

Mṛcchakaṭikā *see* **Śūdraka.**

Mṛgāṅkalekhā *see* **Viśvanātha.**

Mṛkṣā L. app. p. 79.

Muditamadālasa *see* **Kumāranarendrasāha.**

Muditarāghava *see* **Bālakṛṣṇa.**

Mudrārākṣasa *see* **Viśākhadatta.**

Muktācarita A 2. p. 217 = 2 Mss.

Muktipariṇaya *see* **Sundaradeva.**

Mukundānanda *see* **Kāśīpati.**

Mukuṭatāḍitaka *see* **Bāṇa Bhaṭṭa.**

Muṇḍita *see* **Śivajyotirvid.**

Murāri.

Anargharāghava. *Manuscripts.* A 1. p. 15 = 68 Mss. and 11 Com.; by Tripurāri 1, by Dhaneśvara 2, by Naracandra 3, by Rucipati 4, by Viṣṇu 3, by Haradatta 1, by Harihara 6; verses from it 2; A 2. p. 186 = 1 Ms. and Com. by Rucipati 1, by Viṣṇu 1; A 3. p. 4 = 14 Mss. and Com. by Rucipati 7, by Lakṣmīdhara 1, by Viṣṇu 2, by Harihara 1; CS. 214, 215, 216; CBMMS. 256; SCBen. 436; Hz. 3. 1601; IO. 7. 4151, 4152, 4153, 4154, 4155; Com. by Rāmānandāśrama, Hz. 3. 1602; by Harihara, Hz. 3. 1603; by Rucipati, CS. 217, 218, Hz. 3. 2019, IO. 7. 4156, 4157. Analyzed by Wilson, 2, pp. 375–383.

Text Editions. Anargharāghava. Edited with occasional notes by P. Tarkavāgīśa. Calcutta, 1860, pp. 242.

Anargharāghava. Madras, 1870, pp. 114.

Anargharāghava. Edited by J. Vidyāsāgara. Calcutta, 1875, pp. 178.

Anargharāghava. With the commentary of Rucipati. Edited by Durgāprasāda and Parab. 1° ed., Bombay, 1887, pp. 3 + 321; 2° ed., 1894, pp. 3 + 321. Kāvyamālā, no. 5.

Anargharāghava. Sanskrit text, edited with a commentary by Lakṣmaṇa Sūri. Tañjanagara, 1900, pp. 345.

Murārivijaya *see* **Jīvarāma** *and* **Śeṣakṛṣṇa.**

N

Nāgānanda *see* **Harṣadeva.**
Nāgarāja A 1. p. 283.
Nāgayya Kuṇḍamālā A 1. p. 109.
Nagnabhūpatigraha A 1. p. 274.
Naiṣadhānanda *see* **Kṣemīśvara.**
Nalabhūmipālarūpaka A 1. p. 280.
Nalacaritra *see* **Nīlakaṇṭha Dīkṣita.**
Nalānanda *see* **Jīvavibudha.**
Nalavilāsa *see* **Rāmacandra.**
Nallādīkṣita Cittavṛttikalyāṇa A 1. p. 186.
Idem Jīvanmuktikalyāṇa A 1. p. 207.
Nandighoṣavijaya *see* **Śivanārāyaṇadāsa.**
Narakāsuravijaya, Narakāsuravadha, Narakāsuradhvaṃsa, *or* Narakadhvaṃsa *see* **Dharma Paṇḍita.**
Narasiṃha Miśra Śivanārāyaṇabhañjamahodaya A 3. p. 134.
Nārāyaṇa Kamalākaṇṭhīrava A 1. p. 79.
Nārāyaṇa Bhaṭṭa Jānakīpariṇaya A 1. p. 206.

Nārāyaṇa Bhaṭṭa.

Veṇīsaṃhāra *or* Veṇīsaṃvaraṇa. *Manuscripts.* A 1. p. 603 = 40 Mss. and 2 Com.; by Jagaddhara 4; A 2. pp. 144, 227 = 3 Mss. and Com. by Jagaddhara 3; A 3. p. 126 = 7 Mss.; CBMMS. 276; SCBen. 995; Hz. 3. 2017; IO. 7. 4171, 4172; TT. 58; Com. by Jagaddhara, IO. 7. 4173. Analyzed by Wilson, 2, pp. 335–344.

Text Editions. Veṇīsaṃhāra. Edited with a preface in English by Muktārām Vidyābāgish. Calcutta, 1855, pp. 21 + 124.

Veṇīsaṃhāra. Poona, 1856, pp. 69.

Veṇīsaṃhāra. Edited with J. Tarkālaṃkāra's commentary. Calcutta, 1867, pp. 252.

Veṇīsaṃhāra. Edited with a commentary by T. Tarkavācaspati. Calcutta, 1868, pp. 10 + 262. Another ed., 1893, pp. 192.

Veṇīsaṃhāra. With the commentary of C. R. Tivari. Benares, 1868.

Veṇīsaṃhāra. Edited with notes and explanations by K. N. Tarkaratna. Calcutta, 1870, pp. 272. In Majumdār's Series.

Veṇīsaṃhāra. Die Ehrenrettung der Königin. Kritisch mit Einleitung und Noten herausgegeben von J. Grill. Leipzig, 1871.

Veṇīsaṃhāra with the commentary of Tarkavācaspati. Edited by J. Vidyāsāgara. Rev. ed., Calcutta, 1875, pp. 205; another ed., 1886.

Veṇīsaṃhāra. Edited by Tirumalatātācārya. Mysore, 1889, pp. 209.

Veṇīsaṃhāra. Edited with the commentary of Jagaddhara, two prefatory notes by L. R. Vaidya, and English notes by N. B. Godabole. Poona, 1895, pp. 324.

Veṇīsaṃhāra. Edited by B. T. and S. T. Dravid. Poona, 1896, pp. 272.

Veṇīsaṃhāra. Edited by K. P. Parab and K. R. Māḍgāvkar. Bombay, 1898, pp. 218.

Veṇīsaṃhāra. Sanskrit text with a commentary by Lakṣmaṇasūri. Cennanagar, no date, pp. 195.

Translation. Veṇīsaṃhāra, a Sanskrit drama, done into English by S. M. Tagore. Calcutta, 1880.

Nārāyaṇa Kavi Candrakalā A 1. p. 179.

Nārāyaṇa Śāstrin Jaitrajaivātṛka. The Victorious Moon. An original play in seven acts. Chilambaram, 1888, pp. 68.

Idem Maithilīya, a drama on the life of Sītā at Maithila; in ten acts. Madras, 1884, pp. 118.

Idem Śarmiṣṭhāvijaya. A drama in four acts on the legend of Śarmiṣṭhā and Yayāti. Madras, 1884, pp. 72.

Idem Sūramayūra. An original drama in seven acts. Chilambaram, 1888, pp. 57.

Nārāyaṇatīrtha Kṛṣṇalīlātaraṅgiṇī A 1. p. 123.

Nārāyaṇavilāsa A 2. p. 63.

Nārāyaṇīvilāsa A 1. p. 294.

Nārāyaṇīvilāsa *see* **Virūpākṣa.**

Narmavatī nāṭyarāsaka mentioned in SD. 543.

Naṭakamelaka prahasana mentioned in SD. 111, 207, 537. *See also* Laṭakamelaka.

Nāṭavāṭa *see* **Yadunandana.**

Nāṭyapariśiṣṭa *see* **Kṛṣṇānanda.**

Navagrahacarita *see* **Ghanaśyāma.**

Navamālikā A 2. p. 61.

Navamālikā *see* **Viśveśvara.**

Nayacandra Rambhāmañjarī nāṭikā A 1. p. 493 = 2 Mss. and 1 Com.

Idem Rambhāmañjarī. Edited by R. D. Śāstri. Bombay, 1890, pp. 86.

Nīlakaṇṭha Dīkṣita Nalacaritra A 1. p. 280; A 2. p. 60.

Nīlāpariṇaya *see* **Dṛgbhavat.**

Nirbhayabhīma *see* **Rāmacandra Mahākavi.**

Nirdoṣadaśaratha cf. L. app. p. 76.

Nṛsiṃha Śṛṅgārastabaka bhāṇa A 1. p. 661.

Nṛsiṃha Bhaṭṭa Hariharānusaraṇayātrā A 1. p. 763.

Nṛsiṃha Kavi Candrakalāpariṇaya *or* Candrakalākalyāṇa A 3. p. 38.

P

Palāṇḍumaṇḍana prahasana A 1. p. 330.

Pañcabāṇavijaya *see* **Raṅgācārya.**

Pañcabāṇavilāsa bhāṇa A 1. p. 315.

Pañcāyudhaprapañca *see* **Trivikrama.**

Pāṇḍavābhyudaya *see* **Rāmadeva.**

Pāṇḍavānanda quoted by Dhanika on DR. 3. 12.

Paravastu Veṅkaṭaraṅga (beginning of nineteenth century) Mañjulanaiṣadha nāṭaka. Printed in Granthapradarśinī (A 3. p. 90).

Pārijāta *see* **Kumāratātaya.**

Pārijātaharaṇa *see* **Gopāladāsa** *and* **Umāpatidhara.**

Pārthaparākrama *see* **Yuvarāja.**

Pārvatīpariṇaya *see* **Bāṇa Bhaṭṭa.**

Pārvatīsvayaṃvara A 1. p. 336.
Pāṣaṇḍaviḍambana prahasana cf. A 1. p. 336.
Payodhimathana prahasana mentioned in RS.
Periyappā Śṛṅgāramañjarīśāharājīya A 2. p. 158.
Peru Sūri Vasumaṅgalā A 2. p. 131.
Prabhāvatīpariṇaya *see* **Harihara** *and* **Viśvanātha Kavirāja.**
Prabhāvatīpradyumna *see* **Rāmakṛṣṇa.**
Prabodhacandrodaya *see* **Kṛṣṇamiśra.**
Pracaṇḍabhairava *see* **Sadāśiva.**
Pracaṇḍagaruḍa vyāyoga A 2. p. 77.
Pracaṇḍapāṇḍava *see* **Rājaśekhara.**
Pracaṇḍarāhūdaya *see* **Ghanaśyāma.**
Pradyumna, a poet and playwright, A 1. p. 352.
Pradyumnābhyudaya A 1. p. 352.
Pradyumnānanda *see* **Veṅkaṭācārya.**
Pradyumnavijaya *see* **Śaṅkara Dīkṣita.**
Prahasana A 1. p. 360 = 4 Mss.; A 3. p. 77.
Prahasana *see* **Kālidāsa.**
Prahlādacarita mentioned in DR. intr. p. 30.
Pramāṇādarśa *see* **Śukleśvara.**
Prasannacaṇḍikā A 1. p. 359.
Prasannarāghava *see* **Jayadeva.**
Pratāparudrakalyāṇa *see* **Vidyānātha.**
Pratāpavilāsa *see* **Gaṅgādhara.**
Priyadarśikā *see* **Harṣadeva.**
Purañjana *see* **Haridāsa.**
Purañjanacarita *see* **Kṛṣṇadatta.**
Pūrṇapuruṣārthacandra *see* **Jātavedas.**
Puruṣottama Dīkṣita Revatīhālānta A 1. p. 534.
Puṣpabhūṣita prakaraṇa mentioned in SD. 511.
Puṣpadūṣitaka prakaraṇa mentioned by Dhanika on DR. 3. 38.
Puṣpamālā *see* **Candraśekhara.**

R

Rādhāmādhava A 2. p. 220 = 2 Mss.
Rāghavābhyudaya quoted in SD. 498.

Rāghavābhyudaya *see* **Bhagavantarāya, Gaṅgādhara, Rāmacandra,** *and* **Veṅkaṭeśvara.**

Rāghavānanda, a dramatist, quoted in SD. 120.

Raghunāthācārya Subhadrāpariṇaya A 1. p. 728 = 2 Mss.

Raghunāthavilāsa *see* **Yajñanārāyaṇa.**

Raghuvilāsa (Raghuvilāpa) *see* **Rāmacandra.**

Raivatamadanikā goṣṭhī mentioned in SD. 541.

Rājacūḍāmaṇi *see* **Cūḍāmaṇi.**

Rājaśekhara, son of Durduka,
also called Rajanīvallabha (A 1. p. 777).

Bālabhārata *see* Pracaṇḍapāṇḍava.

Bālarāmāyaṇa mahānāṭaka. *Manuscripts.* A 1. p. 372 = 13 Mss. and 1 Com.; Hz. 3. 1572.

Text Editions. Bālarāmāyaṇa. Edited by G. D. Śāstri. Benares, 1869, pp. 324. In The Pandit, old series, 3, nos. 25–35.

Bālarāmāyaṇa, edited with a commentary by J. Vidyāsāgara. Calcutta, 1884, pp. 103.

Bālarāmāyaṇa. Sanskrit text with a commentary by Lakṣmaṇa Sūri. Tanjanagara, 1899, pp. 198.

Karpūramañjarī saṭṭaka. *Manuscripts.* A 1. p. 82 = 22 Mss. and 5 Com.; by Kāmarāja 1, by Kṛṣṇasūnu 1, by Dharmadāsa 1, by Pītāmbara 2 (cf. A 1. p. 491), by Vāsudeva 2; A 2. pp. 15, 191 = 5 Mss. and Com. by Dharmacandra 1, by Vāsudeva 3; A 3. p. 18 = 7 Mss. and 1 Com.; IO. 7. 4162, 4163. See also Konow and Lanman's edition, pp. xxiii–xxvi.

Text Editions. Karpūramañjarī. Edited by Vāmanācārya. Benares, 1872–1873. In The Pandit, old series, 7, nos. 73–76.

Karpūramañjarī. Benares, 1883.

Karpūramañjarī, with the commentary of Vāsudeva. Edited by Durgāprasāda and Parab. Bombay, 1887, pp. 121. In Kāvyamālā, no. 4.

Karpūramañjarī. Edited with a full commentary by J. Vidyāsāgara. Calcutta, 1889, pp. 160.

Karpūramañjarī. A Lucky Wife. Composed from Prakrita or Maharashtri dialect. By V. S. Islampurkar. Bombay, 1890.

Karpūramañjarī. A drama by the Indian poet Rājaśekhara (about 900 A. D.), critically edited in the original Prākrit with a glossarial index and an essay on the life and writings of the poet by Sten Konow and translated into English by C. R. Lanman. Cambridge, Mass., 1901, pp. 26 + 289. Harvard Oriental Series, vol. 4.

Criticism. Cimmino, Francesco. Studii sul teatro indiano. 1. Sul dramma Karpūramañjarī. In Rendiconto dell' Accademia di Archeologia, Lettere e Belle Arti (di Napoli), 19 (1905), pp. 1–30.

Pracaṇḍapāṇḍava *or* Bālabhārata. *Manuscripts.* A 1. p. 348 = 4 Mss. Analyzed by Wilson, 2, pp. 361–362.

Text Editions. Pracaṇḍapāṇḍava, zum ersten Male herausgegeben von Carl Cappeller. Strassburg, 1885, pp. 9 + 50.

Bālabhārata. Edited by Durgāprasāda and Parab. Bombay, 1887, pp. 36. In Kāvyamālā, no. 4.

Viddhaśālabhañjikā nāṭikā. *Manuscripts.* A 1. p. 573 = 9 Mss. and Com. by Nārāyaṇa 1; A 2. p. 135 = 4 Mss. and Com. by Nārāyaṇa 2; A 3. p. 121 = 3 Mss. and Com. by Ghanaśyama 1; Com. by Ghanaśyāma, Hz. 3. 1677; Com. by Sundarī and Kamalā (wives of Ghanaśyāma), Hz. 3. 1676. Analyzed by Wilson, 2, pp. 354–360.

Text Editions. Viddhaśālabhañjikā. Edited by Vāmanācārya. Benares, 1872–1873. In The Pandit, old series, 6–7, nos. 65–73.

Biddhashala Bhanjika, with a commentary by Satyabrata Samasrami. Edited by J. Vidyāsāgara. Calcutta, 1873, pp. 99.

Biddhashalabhanjika. Edited with a commentary by J. Vidyāsāgara. Calcutta, 1883, pp. 150.

Viddhaśālabhañjikā, with the commentary of Nārāyaṇa, edited with explanatory and critical notes, various readings, and a glossary by B. R. Arte. To which is added the Ṛtusaṃhāra of Kālidāsa. Poona, 1886, pp. 156 + 48.

Translation. The Viddhaśālabhañjikā of Rājaśekhara, now first translated from the Sanskrit and Prākrit by Louis H. Gray. In JAOS. 27 (1906). [In press.]

General Criticism of Rājaśekhara. Apte, V. S: Rājaśekhara, his Life and Writings. Poona, 1886, pp. 54.

Fleet, J. F. The Date of the Poet Rājaśekhara. In IA. 16 (1887), pp. 175–178.

Kielhorn, F. On the Date of Rājaśekhara. In Ep. Ind. 1 (1889), pp. 162–179.

Rājimatiprabodha *see* **Yaśaścandra.**

Rāma Manmathonmathana ḍima A 2. p. 99.

Rāmabhadra Śṛṅgārataraṅgiṇī bhāṇa A 1. p. 660.

Rāmabhadra Dīkṣita, called Cokkanātha, (17th century) Jānakīpariṇaya A 1. p. 206 = 51 Mss.; A 2. p. 42 = 2 Mss.

Idem Jānakīpariṇaya, a drama in seven acts on the Sītā legend. With a Marathi translation by G. S. L. Tryambakar, and with an appendix containing a Sanskrit version of the Prākrit passages. Bombay, 1866, pp. 479 + 20.

Idem Jānakīpariṇaya. Madras, 1883, pp. 155.

Idem Śṛṅgāratilaka bhāṇa A 1. p. 660 = 6 Mss. and Com. by Rāmacandra 1.

Idem Śṛṅgāratilaka bhāṇa. Edited by Śivadatta and Parab. Bombay, 1894, pp. 5 + 58. Kāvyamālā, no. 44.

Rāma Bhaṭṭa Madālasa A 1. p. 426. Called Ujjīvitamadālasa in DR. intr. p. 30.

Rāmābhinanda mentioned in SD. 308. *See also* Rāmānanda.

Rāmābhyudaya *see* **Rāmadeva** *and* **Yaśovarman.**

Rāmacandra Nalavilāsa A 3. p. 60.

Idem Rāghavābhyudaya A 3. p. 107.

Idem Raghuvilāsa A 3. p. 104; (Raghuvilāpa) A 1. p. 487.

Idem Yādavābhyudaya A 3. p. 102.

Rāmacandra Sarasakavikulānanda bhāṇa A 1. p. 699.

Rāmacandra Satya Hariścandra Nāṭaka. Edited in Sanskrit by B. R. Arte and Ś. V. Purāṇik. Bombay, 1898, pp. 61.

Rāmacandra (wrote before 1588) Vāsantikā nāṭikā A 1. p. 556 (Vasantikā); A 3. p. 120 = IO. 7. 4186 (not 4136).

Rāmacandra Dīkṣita Keralābharaṇa bhāṇa A 1. p. 125 = 2 Mss.

Rāmacandra Kavi (end of 18th century) Aindavānanda A 1. p. 76.

Idem Kalānanda A 1. p. 84.

Rāmacandra Mahākavi Nirbhayabhīma vyāyoga A 1. p. 298.

Rāmacandra *see also* **Rāmavarman.**

Ramacandranāṭaka A 1. p. 513.

Rāmacarita A 1. p. 514.

Rāmadeva *or* **Vyāsa Śrī Rāmadeva** (15th century) Pāṇḍavābhyudaya chāyānāṭaka A 3. p. 161 = IO. 7. 4187 (copied in 1471); L. app. p. 77.

Idem Rāmābhyudaya chāyānāṭaka A 2. pp. 122, 221; CBMMS. 272. Cf. Bendall in JRAS. 1898, p. 231.

Idem Subhadrāpariṇaya chāyānāṭaka A 1. p. 728; CBMMS. 271.

Rāma Kavi Madanagopālavilāsa bhāṇa A 1. p. 425; A 2. p. 97.

Rāmakṛṣṇa Sūri, son of Āhlāda, Prabhāvatīpradyumna A 2. p. 79 = 2 Mss.

Rāmamāṇika Kavirāja Kṛtārthamādhava A 3. p. 25.

Rāmānanda mentioned in Rucipati's commentary on the Anargarāghava of Murāri (ed. of Durgāprasāda and Parab, p. 70). Same as Rāmābhinanda.

Rāmānanda Rāya (end of 15th century) Jagannāthavallabha A 1. p. 196 = 2 Mss.; A 2. p. 200; A 3. p. 43.

Idem Jagannāthavallabha. A dramatic poem on the adventures of Kṛṣṇa at Vṛndāvan, with a Bengali translation by R. Vidyāratna. 2° ed. Murshidabad, 1882, pp. 116.

Rāmanāṭaka A 1. p. 515 = 3 Mss.; A 2. p. 121.

Rāmāṅka *see* **Dharmagupta.**

Rāmānuja Kavi Vivekavijaya A 2. p. 137.

Rāmasukaviśekhara Śṛṅgārarasodaya miśrabhāṇa A 2. p. 158.

Rāmavarman Yuvarāja *or* **Rāmacandra** (1755–1787) Rukmiṇīpariṇaya A 1. p. 527 = 2 Mss.

Idem Rukmiṇīpariṇaya. Edited by Śivadatta and Parab. Bombay, 1894, pp. 3 + 52. Kāvyamālā, no. 40.

Idem Śṛṅgārasudhākara bhāṇa mentioned in Kāvyamālā, no. 40, p. 1 (A 2. p. 158).

Rāmāyaṇanāṭaka *see* **Someśvaradeva.**

Rambhāmañjarī *see* **Nayacandra.**

Rāmila, a playwright. Cf. F. Hall, Fragments of three early Hindu dramatists, in JASBe. 28 (1859), pp. 28–30.

Rāmmoy Vidyābhūṣaṇa Devadurgatī prahasana. Calcutta, 1884, pp. 14.

Rāmodaya *see* **Śrīvatsalāñchana.**

Raṅgācārya Pañcabāṇavijaya bhāṇa A 1. p. 315 = 7 Mss.

Idem Pañcabāṇavijaya, or the conquest of the love-god, a bhāṇa or dramatic monologue. Edited by V. R. Cārlu. 1° ed., Madras, 1882, pp. 48; 2° ed., 1886, pp. 46.

Raṅgadatta mentioned in SD. 512. *See also* Taraṅgadatta.

Raṅganātha Śṛṅgāraśṛṅgāṭaka bhāṇa A 2. p. 158.

Raṅganātha (?) A 1. p. 488.

Rasasadana *see* **Yuvarāja.**

Rasavilāsa *see* **Cokkanātha.**

Rasikajanarasollāsa *see* **Veṅkaṭa.**

Rasikāmṛta *see* **Śaṅkara Nārāyaṇa.**

Rasikarañjana *see* **Śrīnivāsācārya.**

Rasollāsa *see* **Śrīnivāsa Vedāntācārya.**

Ratimanmatha *see* **Jagannātha Paṇḍita.**

Ratnaketūdaya A 1. p. 489 = 2 Mss.

Ratnakheṭa Dīkṣita Bhaimīpariṇaya A 1. p. 416 = 2 Mss.

Ratnāvalī *see* **Harṣadeva.**

Ravidāsa Mithyājñānaviḍambana *or* Mithyājñānakhaṇḍana A 1. p. 455 = 3 Mss.; A 2. p. 105 = 2 Mss.; A 3. p. 98 = 2 Mss.; IO. 7. 4200 (Analyzed).

Idem Mithyājñānaviḍambana. Calcutta, 1885, pp. 25.

Revatīhālānta *see* **Puruṣottama.**

Rudracandradeva *or* **Rudradeva** Uṣārāgodaya nāṭikā A 1. p. 71 = 6 Mss. and 1 Com.; IO. 7. 4174. Analyzed by R. Mitra, Notices of Sanskrit Manuscripts, 3, p. 192.

Idem Yayāticarita A 1. p. 473 = 2 Mss. Analyzed by Wilson, 2, pp. 388–389.

Rudraśarman Tripāṭhin Caṇḍīvilāsa *or* Caṇḍīcarita A 1. p. 177 = 5 Mss. (with Com. by the author).

Rukmiṇī *see* **Sarasvatīnivāsa.**

Rukmiṇīharaṇa *see* **Śeṣacintāmaṇi.**

Rukmiṇīkalyāṇa *see* **Cūḍāmaṇi Dīkṣita.**

Rukmiṇīpariṇaya *see* **Kavitārkikasiṃha, Rāmavarman,** *and* **Varada Kavi.**

Rūpa Gosvāmin (end of 15th century) Dānakeli *or* Dānakelikaumudī bhāṇikā A 1. p. 249 = 2 Mss. and 1 Com.; A 2. pp. 53, 205 = 2 Mss. and Com. by Jīvagosvāmin 1. A 3. p. 54 = 3 Mss. and Com. by Raghunāthadāsa 1.

Idem Dānakelikaumudī, a play founded on Vaiṣṇava legends, with a commentary by Jīva Gosvāmin, and a Bengali translation by R. Vidyāratna. In Vaiṣṇavadharmaprakāśikā, parts 1–6, Murshidabad (Berhampur), 1881.

Idem Lalitamādhava A 1. p. 542 = 4 Mss.; A 2. p. 128; A 3. p. 115 = 2 Mss. and Com. by Nārāyaṇa 1; IO. 7. 4179.

Idem Vidagdhamādhava (composed in 1533) A 1. p. 572 = 9 Mss. and 1 Com.; A 2. pp. 135, 225 = 3 Mss. and 1 Com.; A 3. p. 121 = 4 Mss. and 1 Com.; IO. 7. 4177, 4178. Analyzed by Wilson, 2, pp. 393–394.

Idem Vidagdhamādhava, a Vaiṣṇava play, with a commentary by V. Cakravarti and a Bengali prose translation by R. Vidyāratna. In Vaiṣṇavadharmaprakāśikā, parts 7–17, Murshidabad (Berhampur), 1882.

Idem Vidagdhamādhava. Edited by Śāstrī and Parab. Bombay, 1903, pp. 3 + 219 + 6. Kāvyamālā, no. 81.

S

Sabhā *see* **Māheśvara.**

Sabhāpativilāsa *see* **Dharmarāja.**

Sadāśiva Pracaṇḍabhairava vyāyoga A 1. p. 348.

Śakuntalā *see* **Kālidāsa.**

Sāmarāja Dīkṣita, son of Narahari Dīkṣita, Dhūrtanartaka A 1. p. 272 = 2 Mss. Analyzed by Wilson, 2, p. 407.

Idem Śrīdāmacarita *or* Dāmacarita (written in 1681) A 1. p. 250; A 2. p. 160; A 3. p. 54. Analyzed by Wilson, 2, pp. 404–406.

Sāmavata *see* **Ambikādatta.**

Samayasāra *see* **Amṛtacandra.**

Saṃkalpasūryodaya A 1. p. 683 = 33 Mss. and 1 Com.; A 2. p. 163 = 1 Ms. and 1 Com.; A 3. p. 142 = 4 Mss. and 1 Com.

Saṃkalpasūryodaya *see* **Veṅkaṭanātha.**

Samṛddhamādhava *see* **Govinda Kavibhūṣaṇa.**

Samudrama(n)thana samavakāra or subject of a samavakāra mentioned in SD. 516 and by Dhanika on DR. 3. 61.

Saṃvaraṇa A 1. p. 681.

Sānandagovinda A 1. p. 707.

Sānandagovinda *see* **Gopāla Bhaṭṭa.**

Sāndrakutūhala *see* **Kṛṣṇadatta.**

Śaṅkara Śāradātilaka bhāṇa A 1. p. 642 = 3 Mss.; A 3. p. 133. Analyzed by Wilson, 2, pp. 384–387.

Śaṅkaradeva Vidagdhamādhava A 2. p. 135.

Śaṅkara Dīkṣita (latter half of eighteenth century), son of Bālakṛṣṇa, Pradyumnavijaya A 1. p. 352 = 3 Mss. Analyzed by Wilson, 2, pp. 402–403.

Śaṅkara Miśra Gaurīdigambara A 3. p. 37.

Śaṅkara Nārāyaṇa Rasikāmṛta A 3. p. 106.

Śaṅkhadhara Laṭakamelaka prahasana A 1. p. 542 = 3 Mss.; A 2. pp. 128, 223 = 5 Mss.; A 3. p. 115.

Idem Laṭakamelaka. Edited by Durgāprasāda and Parab. Bombay, 1889, pp. 3 + 30. Kāvyamālā, no. 20.

Ṣaṇmata *see* **Jayanta.**

Śānticaritra, a Buddhist play, cf. L. app. p. 81.
Śāntirasa *see* **Vaikuṇṭhapurī.**
Śāradānanda bhāṇa A 2. p. 152.
Śāradātilaka *see* **Śaṅkara.**
Sarasakavikulānanda *see* **Rāmacandra.**
Sārasvatādarśa *see* **Appāśāstrin.**
Sarasvatīnivāsa Rukmiṇīnāṭaka A 1. p. 527.
Śarmiṇiṣṭha *see* **Maikela.**
Śarmiṣṭhāvijaya *see* **Nārāyaṇa Śāstrin.**
Śarmiṣṭhāyayāti utsṛṣṭikāṅka mentioned in SD. 519.
Śarmiṣṭhāyayāti *see* **Bhāgavata.**
Śārṅgadhara Śārṅgadharīya A 1. p. 643 = 2 Mss.
Sarvacarita *see* **Bāṇa Bhaṭṭa.**
Śaṭhakopācārya Bhaimīpariṇaya A 2. p. 95.
Satsaṅgavijaya *see* **Vaidyanātha.**
Satyabhāmāvilāsa *see* **Kṛṣṇakavīndra.**
Satyahariścandra *see* **Rāmacandra.**
Saugandhikāharaṇa vyāyoga A 1. p. 737; mentioned in SD. 514.
Saugandhikāharaṇa *see* **Viśvanātha.**
Saugandhikāpariṇaya A 1. p. 737.
Saumillaka *see* **Somila.**
Saumyasomābhidha *see* **Śrīnivāsa.**
Sāvitrīcarita *see* **Maheśvarātmaja.**
Śeṣacintāmaṇi (wrote before 1675), son of Nṛsiṃha, Rukmiṇīharaṇa A 1. p. 527 = 2 Mss.; CBMMS. 274.
Idem Strijñan Dipak. A metrical translation into Gujarati of the Rukmiṇīharaṇa. Bombay, 1873, pp. 296.
Śeṣakṛṣṇa, also called Kṛṣṇa or Kṛṣṇakavi (end of the 16th century), son of Nṛsiṃha or Narasiṃha, Kaṃsavadha A 1. p. 77 = 14 Mss. and 4 Com.; A 2. p. 15; A 3. p. 17 = 2 Mss.; SCBen. 299; Hz. 3. 2080; IO. 7. 4175, 4176. Analyzed by Wilson, 2, pp. 400–402.
Idem Kaṃsavadha. Edited by Durgāprasāda and Parab. Bombay, 1888, pp. 3 + 80. Kāvyamālā, no. 6.
Idem Murārivijaya A 1. p. 462 = 3 Mss.; A 2. p. 106.

Sevantikāpariṇaya A 1. p. 734 = 3 Mss.
Shahji, king of Tanjore (1684–1711), Candraśekharavilāsa A 1. p. 182.
Ṣitalacandra Vidyābhūṣaṇa Goṣayātrā. A play in ten acts on the story of Duryodhana. Calcutta, 1885, pp. 4 + 41.
Sītānanda *see* **Tātārya.**
Sītārāghava A 1. p. 723.
Sītārāma Jānakīpariṇaya A 1. p. 206.
Sītāsvayaṃvara *see* **Hanuman.**
Sītāvivāha A 1. p. 723.
Śivabhaktānanda A 1. p. 650.
Śivajyotirvid Muṇḍita prahasana A 1. p. 461 = 2 Mss.
Śivanārāyaṇabhañjamahodaya *see* **Narasiṃha.**
Śivanārāyaṇadāsa Nandighoṣavijaya *or* Kamalāvilāsa A 1. p. 276 ; A 3. p. 161 = IO. 7. 4190.
Śivanātha Śarman, a playwright. Cf. A. W. Ryder in JAOS. 23 (1902), p. 79.
Śivasvāmin (second half of the 9th century) a playright of Kashmir (L. app. p. 87).
Somadeva Lalitavigraharājanāṭaka. A portion was edited by Kielhorn in IA. 20 (1891), pp. 201–212.
Somavallīyogānanda *see* **Aruṇagirinātha** *and* **Ḍiṇḍima.**
Somayājin *see* **Mallāsomayājin.**
Someśvaradeva Rāmāyaṇanāṭaka A 1. p. 524 = 2 Mss.
Somila, a playwright. Cf. F. Hall, Fragments of three early Hindu dramatists, in JASBe. 28 (1859), pp. 28–30.
Śrīdāmacarita *see* **Sāmarāja.**
Śrīkaṇṭha Kandarpadarpaṇa Hz. 3. 1683.
Śrīnivāsa Saumyasomābhidha, a modern drama in four acts. Chilambaram, 1887, pp. 80.
Śrīnivāsācārya Sudarśanavijaya A 1. p. 724.
Śrīnivāsācārya Uṣāpariṇaya A 1. p. 71.
Śrīnivāsācārya Rasikarañjana bhāṇa. Mysore, 1885, pp. 60.
Śrīnivāsa Catuṣkavīndradāsa, son of Rāmānujasarvakratu, Lakṣmīsvayaṃvara A 1. p. 540 ; A 3. p. 114.
Śrīnivāsadāsa Maratakavallīpariṇaya A 1. p. 433 = 2 Mss.

Śrīnivāsātirātrayājin Bhāvanāpuruṣottama A 1. p. 407 = 2 Mss.

Śrīnivāsa Vedāntācārya Rasollāsa bhāṇa A 1. p. 498.

Śrīraṅgarāja *see* **Gopālarāya.**

Śrīvatsalāñchana Rāmodaya A 1. p. 526.

Śṛṅgārabhūṣaṇa *see* **Vāmana.**

Śṛṅgāracandrikā bhāṇa A 2. p. 157.

Śṛṅgāradīpaka *see* **Veṅkaṭādhvarin.**

Śṛṅgārajīvana bhāṇa A 1. p. 660.

Śṛṅgārakośa *see* **Girvānendra** *and* **Kāśyapa.**

Śṛṅgāramañjarī *see* **Gopālarāya** *and* **Viśveśvara.**

Śṛṅgāramañjarīśāharājīya *see* **Periyappā.**

Śṛṅgārarasodaya *see* **Liṅgaguṇṭamarāma** *and* **Rāmasukaviśekhara.**

Śṛṅgārasarvasva *see* **Cūḍāmaṇi, Kauśika,** *and* **Svāmimiśra.**

Śṛṅgāraśṛṅgāṭaka *see* **Raṅganātha.**

Śṛṅgārastabaka *see* **Nṛsiṃha.**

Śṛṅgārasudhākara *see* **Rāmavarman.**

Śṛṅgārataraṅgiṇī *see* **Rāmabhadra** *and* **Veṅkaṭācārya.**

Śṛṅgāratilaka prasthāna mentioned in SD. 544.

Śṛṅgāratilaka *see* **Rāmabhadra Dīkṣita.**

Śṛṅgāravāpikā *see* **Viśvanātha Bhaṭṭa.**

Stambhitarambha troṭaka mentioned in SD. 540.

Subhadrādhanaṃjaya *see* **Gururāmakavi.**

Subhadrāharaṇa A 1. p. 728 = 2 Mss. and 1 Com.

Subhadrāharaṇa *see* **Mādhava Bhaṭṭa.**

Subhadrāpariṇaya A 1. p. 728.

Subhadrāpariṇaya *see* **Raghunāthācārya** *and* **Rāmadeva.**

Subhadrāvijaya A 1. p. 728.

Subhagānanda prahasana A 1. p. 727.

Subhaṭa Dūtāṅgada chāyānāṭaka A 1. p. 257 = 6 Mss.; A 2. pp. 55, 205 = 5 Mss.; A 3. p. 55; CBMMS. 269; IO. 7. 4188. Another recension, also attributed to Subhaṭa, IO. 7. 4189. Analyzed by Wilson, 2, p. 390, and by Aufrecht, Cat. Codd. Sanscr. Bibl. Bodl., Oxford, 1864, p. 139.

Idem Dūtāṅgada. Edited by Durgāprasāda and Parab. 1° ed., Bombay, 1891, pp. 3 + 15; 2° ed., 1900, pp. 3 + 15. Kāvyamālā, no. 28.

Subrahmaṇya Kavi Vijayendirāpariṇaya A 2. p. 135.

Sudarśanavijaya *see* **Śrīnivāsācārya.**

Śūdraka.

Mṛcchakaṭikā prakaraṇa. *Manuscripts.* A 1. p. 465 = 12 Mss. and 2 Com.; by Gaṇapati 1, by Pṛthvīdhara 5, by Rāmamayaśarman 1, by Lallādīkṣita 1 (made for Wilson); A 2. p. 107 = 2 Mss. and Com. by Pṛthvīdhara 1, by Lallādīkṣita 1; CS. 252, 253, 254; IO. 7. 4123, 4124; Com. by Lallādīkṣita, CS. 251; Com. by Pṛthvīdhara, CS. 255.

Text Editions. Mṛcchakaṭikā, with a commentary explanatory of the Prākrit passages. Calcutta, 1829, pp. 2 + 343.

Mṛcchakaṭikā, id est, Curriculum Figlinum Sūdrakae regis. Fabula sanskrite edidit A. F. Stenzler. Bonn, 1847, pp. 8 + 332.

Mṛcchakaṭikā, edited with a commentary by Rāmamayaśarman and a preface in Bengali by V. Majumdār. Calcutta, 1870, pp. 386. In Majumdār's Series.

Mṛcchakaṭikā, edited with a commentary by J. Vidyāsāgara. 1° ed., Calcutta, 1881, pp. 425; 2° ed., 1891, pp. 351; 3° ed., 1898, pp. 355.

Mṛcchakaṭikā, with the commentaries of Lallādīkṣita and Pṛthvīdhara and various readings. Edited by N. B. Godabole. Bombay, 1896, pp. 594.

Mṛcchakaṭikā, with the commentary of Pṛthvīdhara. Edited by K. P. Parab. Bombay, 1900, pp. 294.

Translations. A. English. The Mṛcchakaṭī, or the Toy-Cart. Translated by Wilson, 1, pp. 1–182.

The Little Clay Cart [Mṛcchakaṭika], a Hindu drama attributed to King Shūdraka, translated from the original Sanskrit and Prākrits into English prose and verse by Arthur W. Ryder. Cambridge, Mass., 1905, pp. 30 + 177. Harvard Oriental Series, vol. 9.

B. French. Le Chariot d'Enfant. Drame en vers, en cinq actes et sept tableaux. Traduction par MM. Méry et G. de Nerval. Paris, 1850.

Mṛcchakaṭikā. Le petit chariot d'argile, drame en dix actes, par H. Fauche. In Une tétrade, ou drame, hymne, roman et poème, traduite pour la première fois du sanscrit en français, vol. 1, Paris, 1861.

Le Chariot de Terre Cuite. Drame sanscrit attribué au roi Çūdraka, traduit et annoté des scolies de Lallā Dīkshita, par Paul Regnaud. Paris, 1876–1877, 4 vols. Bibl. Orient. Elzévir., nos. 6–9.

C. German. Mṛkkhakaṭikā, das ist, das irdene Wägelchen, ein dem König Çūdraka zugeschriebenes Schauspiel. Übersetzt von Otto Böhtlingk. St. Petersburg, 1877, pp. 4 + 213.

Mṛcchakaṭikā; metrisch übersetzt von Ludwig Fritze. In his Indisches Theater, vol. 3, Schloss-Chemnitz, 1879.

Vasantasenā; Drama, mit freier Benutzung der Dichtung des altindischen Königs Sudraka, von Emil Pohl. Stuttgart, 1893, pp. 128.

Vasantasenā, oder das irdene Wägelchen. Freie Übersetzung von Michael Haberlandt. Leipzig, 1893, pp. 20 + 214.

Vasantasenā, oder das irdene Wägelchen. Ein indisches Schauspiel in zehn Aufzügen von König Çūdraka. Deutsch von Hermann Camillo Kellner. 1° ed., Leipzig, 1893, pp. 200; 2° ed., 1894, pp. 199.

D. Dutch. Het Leemen Wagentje, Indisch Tooneelspel, uit Sanskṛt en Prākṛt in het Nederlandsch vertaald door J. Ph. Vogel. Amsterdam, 1897, pp. 15 + 216.

E. Swedish. Vasantasenā. Indiskt drama i 5 akter. Fritt after Emil Pohls tyska bearbetning. Stockholm, 1894, pp. 119.

Mṛcchakaṭikā. Den lilla lervagnen. Ett indiskt skådespel öfversatt av Hilding Andersson. Lund, 1899, pp. 133.

F. Danish. Mṛcchakaṭikā. Lervognen. Et indisk Skuespil. Oversat af E. Brandes. Copenhagen, 1870.

G. Italian. Introduzione alla versione del Mṛcchakaṭikā

(opera di Çūdraka) da Michele Kerbaker. Florence, 1872. [With translation of first act.]

Mṛcchakaṭikā, versione italiana di Michele Kerbaker. Published in part in the Rivista Europea, Florence, Dec. 1869, and in the Giornale Napolitano, new series, 9 (1884), pp. 1–83.

H. Russian. Vasantasenā, drevnaya indĕiskaya drama. Perevod s sanskritskago C. Kossoviča. In Moskvityanin, Moscow, 1849.

Criticism. Boltz, A. Vasantasenā und die Hetären im indischen Drama; Das Vedavolk in seinen Gesamtverhältnissen: Zwei Vorträge. Darmstadt, 1894, pp. 56 [= 'Ἑλλάς, 5 (Leiden, 1894), pp. 279–305].

Cappeller, C. Zur Mṛcchakaṭikā. In Festgruss an O. von Böhtlingk, Stuttgart, 1888, pp. 20–22.

Chaṭṭopādhyāya, N. Three Lectures: The Reminiscences of the German University Life, The True Theosophist, and The Mricchakatikam, or the Toy Cart. Bombay, 1895, pp. 89.

Chaṭṭopādhyāya, N. Mṛcchakaṭikā, or the Toy-Cart of King Śūdraka. A study. Mysore, 1902, pp. 10 + 82.

Kellner, H. C. Einleitende Bemerkungen zu dem indischen Drama Mṛcchakaṭikā. Zwickau, 1872, pp. 28. In Jahresb. d. Gymnasiums zu Zwickau.

Lévi, Sylvain. Le théâtre indien à Paris. In Revue de Paris, 1895, pp. 818–829. [On the production of Barrucand's French version at Paris.]

Nyāyaratna, M. On the Authorship of the Mṛcchakaṭikā. In Proc. of the Asiatic Soc. of Bengal, 1887, pp. 193–200.

Pavolini, P. E. Il Carretto d'Argilla. Conferenza. In Rassegna Nazionale, 24 (Florence, 1902), pp. 586–610.

Ryder, A. W. The Clay Cart. In Boston Transcript, Nov. 21, 1903. [Includes selected passages in translation.]

Wilson, H. H. Sur un drame indien; extrait du Calcutta Annual Register, et traduit par M. Dondey-Dupré fils. In JA. 1° series, 10 (1827), pp. 174–188, 193–209.

Windisch, E. Über das Drama Mṛcchakaṭikā und die Kṛṣṇalegende. In Bericht der phil.-hist. Cl. der Kön. Sächs. Gesells. der Wiss., 4 (1885), pp. 439–479.

Śukla Bhūdeva (16th century) Dharmavijaya A 1. p. 269 = 9 Mss. and Com. by Bhavānīśaṅkara 7; A 2. pp. 58, 206 = 2 Mss. and 1 Com.; A 3. p. 58; IO. 7. 4182, 4183; Com. by Bhavānīśaṅkara, IO. 7. 4183.
Idem Dharmavijaya. Bombay, 1889. In Grantharatnamālā 3.
Śukleśvara Pramāṇādarśa mentioned in DR. intr. p. 30.
Sulocanāvivāha (?) L. app. p. 82.
Sumatijitāmitramalladeva, king of Bhātgāon, Aśvamedha A 3. p. 8.
Sundaradeva, son of Govinda, Muktipariṇaya A 1. p. 459 = 2 Mss.
Sundaradeva Vinodaraṅga prahasana A 1. p. 577.
Sundara Kavi Anaṅgamaṅgala bhāṇa cf. A 1. p. 12.
Sundara Miśra Abhirāmamaṇi (composed in 1599) A 1. p. 26 = 2 Mss. Analyzed by Wilson, 2, p. 395.
Sundara Rāja Vaidarbhīvasudeva, a drama in five acts, on the legend of Rukmiṇī and Kṛṣṇa. Kailāsapura (Tinnevelli), 1888, pp. 6 + 112.
Sūramayūra *see* **Nārāyaṇa Śāstrin.**
Svāmimiśra *or* **Svāmiśāstrin** Śṛṅgārasarvasva A 1. p. 661; A 2. p. 158.
Svānubhūtyabhidha *see* **Anantarāma.**
Svapnadaśānana *see* **Bhīmaṭa.**
Svapnavāsavadattā *see* **Bhāsa.**
Svarṇamuktāvivāda *see* **Maheśa.**

T

Tāpasavatsarāja *see* **Mātrarāja.**
Taraṅgadatta prakaraṇa mentioned by Dhanika on DR. 3. 38. *See also* Raṅgadatta.
Tarkālaṃkāra Mahāmahopādhyāya Kaumudīsudhākara prakaraṇa. Calcutta, 1888, pp. 6 + 217.
Tātārya Sītānanda A 1. p. 723.
Tripuradāha ḍima or subject of a ḍima mentioned in Bharata, 4. 9, and on Bharata's authority in SD. 517 and by Dhanika on DR. 3. 53.

Tripurāri A 1. p. 237.

Trivikrama Paṇḍita Pañcāyudhaprapañca bhāṇa A 1. p. 317 = 5 Mss.; A 2. p. 209.

Tumburunāṭaka mentioned in the Saṃgītadāmodara (L. app. p. 76).

U

Udāttarāghava mentioned in SD. 283, 420, and by Hemacandra (A 1. p. 65). Probably the same work as the Udāttarāghava of **Māyurāja.**

Udāttarāghava *see* **Māyurāja.**

Udayanacarita mentioned in DR. 2. 53 and SD. 422.

Uddaṇḍin (not earlier than the 15th century) Mallikāmāruta prakaraṇa A 1. p. 434 = 5 Mss.

Idem Mallikāmāruta. With the commentary of Raṅganāthācārya. Edited by J. Vidyāsāgara. Calcutta, 1878, pp. 4 + 338.

Ujjīvitamadālasa *see* **Rāma Bhaṭṭa.**

Umāpatidhara (12th century) Pārijātaharaṇa A 1. p. 335.

Unmatta *see* **Veṅkaṭeśa Kavi.**

Unmattarāghava *see* **Bhāskara** *and* **Mahādeva Śāstrin.**

Uṣāharaṇa *see* **Harṣanātha.**

Uṣāpariṇaya *see* **Śrīnivāsācārya.**

Uṣārāgodaya *see* **Rudracandradeva.**

Uttararāmacarita *see* **Bhavabhūti.**

V

Vādicandra Sūri, a Jain, Jñānasūryodaya A 1. p. 210.

Vadhyaśilā quoted in SD. 482.

Vaidarbhīvasudeva *see* **Sundara Rāja.**

Vaidyanātha Kṛṣṇalīlā nāṭikā A 1. p. 123; A 2. pp. 24, 195; CS. 221.

Vaidyanātha Mithyācāra prahasana cf. A 1. p. 455.

Vaidyanātha Satsaṅgavijaya A 1. p. 690 = 2 Mss.

Vaidyanātha Vācaspati Citrayajña A 1. p. 187; CS. 224. Analyzed by Wilson, 2, pp. 412–415.

Vaikuṇṭhapurī Śāntirasa A 2. p. 152.

Vajramukuṭīvilāsa A 1. p. 548 = 3 Mss.
Vakratuṇḍagaṇanāyaka prakaraṇa A 1. p. 547.
Vakulamālinīpariṇaya (?) L. app. p. 80.
Vallīpariṇaya *see* **Vīrarāghava.**
Vāmana Bhaṭṭa Bāṇa Śṛṅgārabhūṣaṇa bhāṇa A 1. p. 661 = 6 Mss.; A 2. p. 158 = 3 Mss.; A 3. p. 137.
Idem Śṛṅgārabhūṣaṇa. Published in Granthapradarśanī (A 3. p. 137).
Idem Śṛṅgārabhūṣaṇa, a dramatic entertainment in one act. Edited by Rāmakṛṣṇa Ācārya. Madras, 1873, pp. 30.
Idem Śṛṅgārabhūṣaṇa. Edited by Śivadatta and Parab. Bombay, 1896, pp. 3 + 19. Kāvyamālā, no. 58.
Vaṃśamaṇi, a Maithila, son of Rāmacandra, Gītadigambara A 3. p. 33.
Vanamāli Miśra Adbhutarāghava A 3. p. 2.
Vāṇībhūṣaṇa *see* **Dāmodara Miśra.**
Varada Anaṅgajīvana *or* Anaṅgasaṃjīvana bhāṇa A 1. p. 12 = 4 Mss.
Varadācārya Ambāla bhāṇa A 1. p. 29.
Varadācārya Anaṅgabrahmavidyāvilāsa bhāṇa cf. A 1. p. 549.
Varadācārya Cola bhāṇa A 2. p. 200.
Varadācārya Vasantatilaka bhāṇa A 1. p. 556 = 34 Mss.; A 2. pp. 131, 224 = 4 Mss.; A 3. p. 118; Hz. 3. 1577; IO. 7. 4198, 4199.
Idem Vasantatilaka. Edited by D. V. Śarman. Calcutta, 1868, pp. 63.
Idem Vasantatilaka. Edited by J. Vidyāsāgara. Calcutta, 1872, pp. 47.
Varadācārya Yatirājavijaya *or* Vedāntavilāsa A 1. p. 471 = 5 Mss. and 1 Com.
Varada Kavi Rukmiṇīpariṇaya A 1. p. 527.
Vasantabhūṣaṇa bhāṇa (?) L. app. p. 80; but cf. A 1. p. 556.
Vasantatilaka *see* **Varadācārya.**
Vāsantikā (Vasantikā) *see* **Rāmacandra.**
Vāsantikāpariṇaya A 1. p. 566 = 3 Mss.; A 2. p. 133.

Vāsantikāpariṇaya *see* **Chaṭa Yati.**
Vāsantikāsvapna *see* **Kṛṣṇamacari.**
Vasumaṅgalā *see* **Peru Sūri.**
Vasumatīcitrasenāvilāsa A 1. p. 557 = 2 Mss.
Vasumatīcitrasenāvilāsa *see* **Appayya.**
Vasumatīpariṇaya *see* **Jagannātha Paṇḍita.**
Vatsarāja Hāsyacūḍāmaṇi prahasana A 1. p. 766.
Vaṭucaritra (?) L. app. p. 80.
Vedakavisvāmin Vidyāpariṇaya A 1. p. 574 = 4 Mss. [This author is said to be the same as **Ānandarāya** (A 2. p. 136).]
Vedāntavāgīśa Bhaṭṭācārya Bhojarājasaccarita *or* Bhojasaccarita A 1. p. 418; A 3. p. 90.
Vedāntavilāsa *see* **Ammāl** *and* **Varadācārya.**
Veṇīsaṃhāra *or* Veṇīsaṃvaraṇa *see* **Nārāyaṇa Bhaṭṭa.**
Veṅkappa Kāmavilāsa bhāṇa A 1. p. 93.
Veṅkaṭa, son of Vedāntadeśika, Rasikajanarasollāsa bhāṇa A 3. p. 106.
Veṅkaṭācārya Bhaimīpariṇaya A 1. p. 416.
Veṅkaṭācārya, of Surapura, Śṛṅgārataraṅgiṇī A 1. p. 660 = 2 Mss.
Veṅkaṭācārya *or* **Veṅkatādhvarin** (also called Araśanipāla) Pradyumnānanda bhāṇa A 1. p. 352 = 3 Mss.; A 2. p. 78.
Veṅkaṭādhvarin Śṛṅgāradīpaka bhāṇa A 1. p. 661.
Veṅkaṭa Kavi, of Kāñcīpura, Kandarpadarpa(ṇa) bhāṇa A 1. p. 79.
Veṅkaṭa Kṛṣṇa Dīkṣita, son of Veṅkaṭādri, Kuśalavavijaya A 2. p. 23.
Veṅkaṭanātha Saṃkalpasūryodaya A 1. p. 683 = 3 Mss. and 1 Com.; by Ahobala 2, by Kauśikakulatilaka 1, by Nārāyaṇa 1, by Rāmānuja 1; A 2. pp. 163, 232 = 3 Mss. and Com. by Ahobala 1.
Idem Saṃkalpasūryodaya, with notes by V. Desikar. Conjevaram, 1883, pp. 372.
Idem Saṃkalpasūryodaya. With a commentary by Śrīnivāsa

Tātayārya and Śaila Tātayārya. The text edited by Kṛṣṇa Tātayācārya. Conjevaram, 1883, pp. 17 + 371.

Veṅkaṭeśa Bhānuprabandha prahasana A 1. p. 405.

Veṅkaṭeśa *see* **Veṅkaṭeśvara.**

Veṅkaṭeśa Kavi Unmatta prahasana A 1. p. 66 = 2 Mss.

Veṅkaṭeśvara Rāghavābhyudaya A 1. p. 500.

Veṅkaṭeśvara Veṅkaṭeśa prahasana A 1. p. 602.

Vibhīṣaṇanirbhartsanāṅka quoted in SD. 477.

Vidagdhamādhava SCBen. 795, 978 (both with Com.).

Vidagdhamādhava *see* **Rūpa Gosvāmin** *and* **Śaṅkaradeva.**

Viddhaśālabhañjikā *see* **Rājaśekhara.**

Vidyānātha Upādhyāya Pratāparudrakalyāṇa cf. A 1. p. 349, L. p. 19.

Vidyānidhi Atandracandrika A 1. p. 6.

Vidyāpariṇaya A 1. p. 574.

Vidyāpariṇaya *see* **Ānandarāya** *and* **Vedakavisvāmin.**

Vigraharājadeva, king of Śākambharī, Harakeli (composed in 1153) cf. F. Kielhorn in IA. 19 (1890), p. 215; 20 (1891), pp. 201–212.

Idem, cf. Kielhorn, F., Sanskrit plays of the King Vigraharājadeva of Śākambharī, partly preserved as inscriptions at Ajmere. In Trübner's Record, 2 (1891), pp. 65–66.

Idem, cf. Kielhorn, F., Bruchstücke des Lalita-Vigraharāja Nāṭaka. In Gött. Nachr. 13 (1893), pp. 552–570.

Vijayapārijāta *see* **Harijīvana.**

Vijayendirāpariṇaya *see* **Subrahmaṇya.**

Vikhyātavijaya *see* **Lakṣmaṇamāṇikyadeva.**

Vikramacandrikā A 1. p. 569.

Vikramorvaśī *see* **Kālidāsa.**

Vikrāntabhīma mentioned by Hemacandra (A 1. p. 569).

Vikrāntaśūdraka mentioned in the Sarasvatīkaṇṭhābharaṇa, p. 378.

Vilakṣakurupati cf. L. app. p. 80.

Vilāsavatī nāṭyarāsaka mentioned in SD. 543.

Viḷināthа Kavi Madanamañjarī A 1. p. 425.

Vinatānanda *see* **Govinda.**

Vindumatī *see* Bindumatī.

Vinodaraṅga *see* **Sundaradeva.**

Vīrabhadravijṛmbhaṇa ḍima mentioned in RS. and in DR. intr. p. 30.

Vīrānanda *see* Mahāvīrānanda.

Vīrarāghava, son of Śrīśailasūri, Indirāpariṇaya Hz. 3. 1749.

Vīrarāghava, son of Īśvara, Vallīpariṇaya A 3. p. 118.

Vīravijaya *see* **Kṛṣṇamiśra.**

Virūpākṣa (circa 1350), son of Bukta, Nārāyaṇīvilāsa A 3. p. 63.

Viśākhadatta.

Mudrārākṣasa nāṭaka. *Manuscripts.* A 1. p. 461 = 43 Mss. and 6 Com.; by Ḍhuṇḍhirāja (composed in 1714) 8, by Maheśvara 1, by Vaṭeśvara 4; A 2. pp. 106, 218 = 9 Mss. and Com. by Graheśvara 1, by Ḍhuṇḍhirāja 2, Prākṛtachāyā by Keśavopādhyāya 1; A 3. p. 99 = 15 Mss. and Com. by Abhirāma 1, by Graheśvara 1, by Ḍhuṇḍhirāja 4; CS. 247, 248, 249; Garbe 188; SCBen. 980; IO. 7. 4165, 4166, 4167, 4168, 4169; Com. by Ḍhuṇḍhirāja, SCBen. 980, Hz. 3. 1666; Com. by Graheśvara, IO. 7. 4170. There is also a prose version by Ananta Paṇḍita, according to A 1. p. 461.

Text Editions. Mudrārākṣasa, a drama in seven acts. With a commentary explanatory of the Prākrit passages. Calcutta, 1831, pp. 157.

Mudrārākṣasa. Edited with notes by T. Tarkavācaspati. Calcutta, 1870, pp. 2 + 231. In Majumdār's Series.

Mudrārākṣasa. With the commentary of Ḍhuṇḍhirāja, part 1. Edited by D. V. Panta. Calcutta, 1873.

Mudrārākṣasa. Edited with a commentary by J. Vidyāsāgara. Calcutta, 1881, pp. 218.

Mudārārkṣasa. With a commentary by Ḍhuṇḍhirāja. Mysore, 1883, pp. 183.

Mudrārākṣasa. With the commentary of Ḍhuṇḍhirāja, edited by K. T. Telang. 1° ed., Bombay, 1884, pp. 54 + 283 + 63; 2° ed., 1893, pp. 375; 3° ed., 1900, pp. 378. Bombay

Sanskrit Series, no. 27. [Cf. also the review by A. Hillebrandt, in ZDMG. 39 (1885), pp. 107–132.]

Mudrārākṣasa. Edited by K. H. Dhruva. Ahmedabad, 1900, pp. 340.

Mudrārākṣasa. Edited with the commentary of Ḍhuṇḍhirāja and an English translation, critical notes, and various readings, by M. R. Kale. Bombay, 1900, pp. 8 + 347.

Translations. A. English. Mudrārākṣasa, or the Signet of the Minister. Translated by Wilson, 2, pp. 125–254.

B. French. Le Sceau de Rākchasa. Drame traduit sur la dernière édition par V. Henry. Paris, 1888, pp. 16 + 237. Collection Orientale, no. 2.

C. German. Mudrarakschasa, oder des Kanzlers Siegelring. Aus dem Sanskrit zum ersten Male und metrisch ins Deutsche übersetzt von Ludwig Fritze. Leipzig, 1886, pp. 133.

D. Italian. Mudrāraxasa, ossia Il Ministro Rassaso vittima del suo sigillo. In Teatro Scelto indiano, tradotto da Antonio Marazzi, vol. 2, Milan, 1874, pp. 1–187.

E. Marathi. Mudrārākṣasa. Translated into Marathi by K. S. Rajvade, revised by K. S. Chiplonkar, edited by S. P. Pandit. Bombay, 1867, pp. 144.

F. Gujarati. Mudrārākṣasa. Translated into Gujarati by K. H. Dhruva. Bombay, 1889, pp. 240.

Criticism. Mudrārākṣasakathāsāra, a poem in 354 stanzas, composed by Ravikartaṇa Sūri to assist readers of the Mudrārākṣasa. With a brief commentary by Rājagopāla of Madura. Madras, 1882, pp. 22.

Mudrārākṣasakathāsāra A 1. p. 461 = 2 Mss.; A 2. p. 106.

Dhruva, K. H. The Age of Viśākhadatta. In WZKM. 5 (1891), pp. 25–35.

Haag, Friedrich. Beiträge zum Verständniss von Viśākhadatta's Mudrāraxasa, mit besonderer Berücksichtigung des Codex Parisinus, part 1. Burgdorf, 1886, pp. 12 + 19.

Jacobi, Hermann. On Viśākhadatta. In WZKM. 2 (1888), pp. 212–216.

Viṣṇukutūhala *see* **Madhusūdana Sarasvatī.**

Viśvanātha, son of Trimaladeva, Mṛgāṅkalekhā nāṭikā A 1. p. 465 ; CS. 256. Analyzed by Wilson, 2, pp. 391–392.

Viśvanātha Saugandhikāharaṇa. Edited by Durgāprasāda and Parab. Bombay, 1902, pp. 3 + 37. Kāvyamālā, no. 74.

Viśvanātha Bhaṭṭa, son of Mahādeva, Śṛṅgāravāpikā nāṭikā A 1. p. 661 ; A 2. p. 158 ; IO. 7. 4196 (Analyzed).

Viśvanātha Kavirāja, author of the Sāhityadarpaṇa, Candrakalā nāṭikā quoted in SD. 447, 465.

Idem Prabhāvatīpariṇaya quoted in SD. 99, 346, 446, 484, 526, 530.

Viśveśvara, son of Lakṣmīdhara, Navamālikā mentioned in Kāvyamālā, part 8 (1891), p. 52.

Idem Śṛṅgāramañjarī saṭṭaka A 2. p. 158.

Viṭṭhala Chāyānāṭaka A 1. p. 193.

Vivekavijaya *see* **Rāmānuja.**

Vṛṣabhānujā *see* **Mathurādāsa.**

Vṛttivallabha *see* **Laghuvyāsa.**

Vyāsa Mokṣāditya *see* **Mokṣāditya.**

Vyāsa Śrī Rāmadeva *see* **Rāmadeva.**

Y

Yādavābhyudaya *see* **Rāmacandra.**

Yādavodaya kāvya mentioned in SD. 546.

Yadunandana, son of Vāsudeva Cayani, Nāṭavāṭa prahasana. Edited in Sanskrit and Prākrit. Bombay, 1887. In Granthāratnamālā, vol. 2, nos. 10–11.

Yajñanārāyaṇa Raghunāthavilāsa A 1. p. 486.

Yaśaścandra, a Jain, Kumudacandra A 1. p. 111.

Idem Rājimatiprabodha cf. L. app. p. 79.

Yaśaḥpāla Moharājaparājaya A 1. p. 468 = 4 Mss. ; A 3. p. 101.

Yaśodhana Dhanaṃjayavijaya vyāyoga A 1. p. 266 = 2 Mss.

Yaśovarman (end of seventh century) Rāmābhyudaya nāṭaka

mentioned in SD. 427 and DR. 1. 42. Cf. ZDMG. 36 (1882), p. 521.

Yatirājavijaya *see* **Varadācārya.**

Yayāticarita *see* **Rudracandradeva.**

Yayātivijaya quoted in SD. 440.

Yogānanda *see* **Aruṇagirinātha** *and* **Ḍiṇḍima.**

Yuvarāja Prahlādana Pārthaparākrama A 1. p. 335 = 3 Mss.

Idem Rasasadana bhāṇa, edited by Śivadatta and Parab. Bombay, 1893, pp. 3 + 65. Kāvyamālā, no. 37.

APPENDIX I

SOME DRAMAS IN THE MODERN VERNACULARS.

Amānat. Indarsabhā, Neuindisches Singspiel in lithographischem Originaltext, mit Übersetzung und Erklärungen, sowie einer Einleitung über das hindustanische Drama, von F. Rosen. Leipzig, 1892, pp. 102 + 64.

Kégl, A. Amánat és a hindusztáni dráma. In Egyetemes philologiai közlöny, 1894, pp. 38–51. [On the Indarsabhā of Amānat.]

Aryotkarṣaka vyāyoga. The regenerator of the Aryas. 1° ed., Surat, 1873, pp. 68; 2° ed., 1888, pp. 68. [In Gujarati.]

Baldeo, K. Bhartṛhari Rāj Tyāj Nāṭak. The drama of Bhartrihari's abdication of the throne. In English (?). Lucknow, 1898.

Bhadranjan. A Hindu drama by a native. No place or date.

Candrahāsa, or, the Lord of the Fair Forger. A Hindu Drama. Mangalore, 1882, pp. 6 + 80.

Dalpatram Dahyabhai. Kavitavilāsa. Ahmedabad, 1870. [In Gujarati.]

Gupta, G. C. Kirti Bilāsa. Bengali drama in five acts. Calcutta, no date, pp. 70.

Hariścandra nāṭakaya, edited by W. G. M. J. de Silva, Colombo, 1901, pp. 104.

Manamohana. Sātī nāṭaka. Benares, 1886, pp. 182.

Rāmabhadra. Lalitakuvalayāśva naṭaka (composed in 1665). Kat. d. Bibl. d. Deutschen Morg. Gesell. 2. p. 6.

Rāmabhadraśarman. Hariścandranṛtya. Kat. d. Bibl. d. Deutschen Morg. Gesell. 2. p. 5.

Rāmabhadraśarman. Das Hariçcandranṛityam. Ein altnepalesisches Tanzspiel. Mit einer grammatischen Einleitung herausgegeben von August Conrady. Leipzig, 1891, pp. 12 + 45.

Rāmacandra. The Satya Harischandra Nāṭaka. Edited by B. R. Arte and S. V. Puranik. Bombay, 1898, pp. 61.

Rāmākṛṣṇa Varman. Padmāvatī nāṭaka. Benares, 1886, pp. 107.

Rāmakṛṣṇa Varman. Kṛṣṇakumārī nāṭaka. Benares, 1899, pp. 156.

Śrīmadgītādarśana, or, a Dramatized Version of the Bhagvatgītā (sic). Edited by A. V. Barve. Bombay, 1903, pp. 48. [In Marathi.]

Tarkālaṃkar, R. C. Kantuk Garbasva Nāṭak. Bengali drama. Calcutta, 1830.

Udayran, R. Premrāyane Cārumati. Bombay, 1876. [In Gujarati.]

Umedcand, C. Okha Haran Natak, or, the drama of the elopement of Okha or Usha. Ahmedabad, 1883, pp. 66. [In Gujarati.]

Vaṃśamaṇi (wrote in Nepal in 1628). Kuvalayāśvamadālasa. Kat. d. Bibl. d. Deutschen Morg. Gesell. 2. p. 7.

Criticism.

Chattopādhyāya, N. The Yātrās, or the popular dramas of Bengal. London, 1882.

Chattopādhyāya, N. Die Yātrās, oder die Volksschauspiele Bengalens. In his Indische Essays, Zürich, 1883, pp. 1–56.

Dennath, G. Bengali Language. In Calcutta Review, 98 (1893), pp. 104–131. [Contains an account of dramas in Bengali.]

Dhruva, H. H. The Rise of the Drama in Modern India. With an Appendix. In Transactions of the 9. Intern. Congr. of Orientalists, London, 1893, vol. 1, pp. 297–314.

Estrey, Count Meyners de. L'Art dramatique dans l'Inde. In Annales de l'extrême Orient, 8 (1885–1886), pp. 289–293.

Haberlandt, M. Das moderne indische Drama. In Öm, 18, pp. 118–121.

Minayev, I. Narodnyya dramatičeskiya predstavleniya v prazdnik Kholi v Almorě. In Zapiski Vostočnago Otděleniya

Imp. Russkago Arkheologičeskago Obščestva, 5 (1891), pp. 290–291.

Oman, J. C. At the Play: The New Indian Theatre. In his Indian Life, London, 1889, pp. 183–199.

Roberts, Sydney. The Kama mystery; a study in comparative dramatics. In Contemporary Review, 115 (1902), pp. 1–9.

Vallet de Viriville, A. Études sur le théatre indien: Stékiare Vassapou. 1845.

APPENDIX II

Classification of the Dramas

A complete classification of the extant dramas according to the divisions (*rūpakas*) and subdivisions (*uparūpakas*) recognized in Indian dramaturgical treatises cannot be made at the present time, because, as pointed out above (p. 3, n. 1), the meagre details of the manuscript catalogues and the ambiguous use of the term *nāṭaka* leave the precise character of many plays still in doubt. Those dramas whose character is definitely known, however, are here grouped under their respective classes, and plays known only by name have also been included, but distinguished from those actually in existence by a prefixed asterisk (*). The authorship of the plays has not been indicated, even in cases where there is more than one work of the same name, as this and other details can easily be ascertained from the corresponding entries in the main body of the work.

Owing to the difficulties of classification pointed out above, very few dramas could with certainty be defined as *nāṭakas* in the narrower sense. In the list there have been included certain others (distinguished by interrogation-points) that seem, for one reason or another, to belong to this group, but cannot be definitely assigned to it at the present time. In spite of these additions, the proportion of plays of this class is much larger than would seem to be indicated by the meagre list here given, and an examination of the large number of dramas vaguely designated as *nāṭakas* would unquestionably disclose many additional productions of this variety.

bhāṇa

Ambāla
Ānandatilaka
Anaṅgabrahmavidyāvilāsa
Anaṅgajīvana
Anaṅgamaṅgala
Anaṅgasarvasva
Anaṅgavijaya
Cola

Gopālalīlārṇava
Harivilāsa
Kāmavilāsa
Kandarpadarpaṇa
Keralābharaṇa
Kusumabāṇavilāsa
* Līlāmadhukara
Madanabhūṣaṇa
Madanagopālavilāsa
Mahiṣamaṅgala
Mālamaṅgalabhāṇa
Miśrabhāṇa
Mukundānanda
Pañcabāṇavijaya
Pañcabāṇavilāsa
Pañcāyudhaprapañca
Pradyumnānanda
Rasasadana
Rasavilāsa
Rasikajanarasollāsa
Rasikarañjana
Rasollāsa
Śāradānanda
Śāradātilaka
Sarasakavikulānanda
Śrīraṅgarāja
Śṛṅgārabhūṣaṇa
Śṛṅgāracandrikā
Śṛṅgāradīpaka
Śṛṅgārajīvana
Śṛṅgārakośa
Śṛṅgāramañjarī
Śṛṅgārasarvasva
Śṛṅgāraśṛṅgāṭaka
Śṛṅgārastabaka
Śṛṅgārasudhākara
Śṛṅgārataraṅgiṇī
Śṛṅgāratilaka
Śṛṅgārarasodaya (*miśrabhāṇa*)
Vasantabhūṣaṇa (?)
Vasantatilaka

bhāṇikā

Dānakelikaumudī
* Kāmadattā

chāyānāṭaka

Chāyānāṭaka
Dūtāṅgada
Haridūta
Pāṇḍavābhyudaya
Rāmābhyudaya
Sāvitrīcarita
Subhadrāpariṇaya

ḍima

Manmathonmathana
* Tripuradāha
* Vīrabhadravijṛmbhaṇa

durmallikā

* Bindumatī

goṣṭhī

* Raivatamadanikā

hallīśa

* Keliraivataka

īhāmṛga

* Kusumaśekharavijaya
* Māyākuraṅgikā

Vīravijaya

kāvya

* Yādavodaya

nāṭaka

Abhijñānaśakuntalā
Amṛtodaya
Bālarāmāyaṇa (*mahānāṭaka*)
Caitanyacandrodaya
Caṇḍakauśika
Jñānasūryodaya (?)
Lalitavigraharājanāṭaka (?)
Mahānāṭaka (*mahānāṭaka*)
Mahāvīracarita
Maṅgala
Mañjulanaiṣadha (?)
Mathurānāṭaka (?)
Mudrārākṣasa
Nāgānanda
Pārvatīpariṇaya
Prasannarāghava
Rāmābhyudaya (?)
Rāmacandranāṭaka (?)
Rāmanāṭaka (?)
Rāmāyaṇanāṭaka (?)
Rukmiṇīnāṭaka (?)
Satyahariścandra
* Tumburunāṭaka (?)
Uttararāmacarita

See the introductory remarks on p. 101.

nāṭikā

* Candrakalā
Candraprabhā
Karṇasundarī
Kṛṣṇalīlā
Kuvalayavatī
Mṛgāṅkalekhā
Priyadarśikā
Rāmāṅka
Rambhāmañjarī
Ratnāvalī
Śṛṅgāravāpikā
Uṣārāgodaya
Vasantikā
Viddhaśālabhañjikā
Vṛṣabhānujā

nāṭyarāsaka

* Narmavatī
* Vilāsavatī

prahasana

Adbhutaraṅga
* Ānandakośa
* Bhagavadajjukā
Bhānuprabandha
* Bṛhatsābhadraka
Devadurgatī
* Dhūrtacarita
Dhūrtasamāgama
Dhūrtaviḍambana
Hāsyacūḍāmaṇi
Hāsyārṇava
Hṛdayavinoda
Kāleyakutūhala
Kālidāsaprahasana
* Kalikeliprahasana
* Kandarpakeli
Kāśīdāsaprahasana
Kautukaratnākara
Kautukasarvasva
Lambodara
Laṭakamelaka
Mithyācāra
Muṇḍita
* Naṭakamelaka
Nāṭavāṭa
Palāṇḍumaṇḍana
Pāṣaṇḍaviḍambana
* Payodhimathana
Prahasana
Sāndrakutūhala
Somavallīyogānanda
Subhagānanda
Unmatta
Veṅkateśa
Vinodaraṅga
Yogānanda

prakaraṇa

* Kāmadatta (*dhūrtaprakaraṇa*)
Kaumudīsudhākara
Mālatīmādhava
Mallikāmāruta
Mṛcchakaṭikā
* Puṣpabhūṣita
* Puṣpadūṣitaka
* Taraṅgadatta
Vakratuṇḍagaṇanāyaka

prasthāna

* Śṛṅgāratilaka

prekṣaṇaka

Kṛṣṇābhyudaya

preṅkhana

* Bālivadha

rāsaka

* Menakāhita

samavakāra

* Samudrama(n)thana

saṃlāpaka

* Māyākāpālika

saṭṭaka

Ānandasundarī
Karpūramañjarī
Śṛṅgāramañjarī

śilpaka

* Kanakāvatīmādhava

śrīgadita

* Krīḍārasātala
Subhadrāharaṇa

troṭaka

* Stambhitarambha
Vikramorvaśī

ullāpya

* Devīmahādeva

utsṛṣṭikāṅka

* Śarmiṣṭhāyayāti

vīthikā

* Mādhavī

vyāyoga

Bhīmavikrama
Dhanaṃjayavijaya
* Jāmadagnyajaya
Narakāsuravijaya
Nirbhayabhīma
Pracaṇḍabhairava
Pracaṇḍagaruḍa
Saugandhikāharaṇa
Vinatānanda